BOOK
ARCHITECTURE

HOW TO PLOT AND OUTLINE WITHOUT USING A FORMULA

STUART HORWITZ

For more information about this title, to book a workshop, or to hire a developmental editor trained in the Book Architecture Method, contact the publisher:

Book Architecture, LLC
One Richmond Square, Suite #112K
Providence, RI 02906
www.BookArchitecture.com
stuart@bookarchitecture.com
Twitter: @Book_Arch
Facebook: www.facebook.com/developmental.editor

ISBN: 978-0-9864204-0-5

Printed in the United States of America

Cover and Interior Graphics: Logica Design
Interior Design: 1106 Design
Editor: Maria Gagliano

"Only in this way can writing be done, only with such coherence, with such a complete opening-out of the body and the soul."

— FRANZ KAFKA

Table of Contents

Series is the New Plot

In *Book Architecture: How to Plot and Outline Without Using a Formula,* you will learn how to create an effective plot and a clear outline for your work-in-progress, whether your work is an advanced draft or you are just starting out, and whether you are working in fiction, film and television, or creative nonfiction. You will learn a new approach to structure, and you won't have to resort to using a formula, which may seem risky! But it can be done.

I founded the company Book Architecture 15 years ago because I was tired of being called a "book doctor"—as if I had some kind of magic pill or syringe I could inject into a manuscript that would cure all of its ills. It doesn't work that way; at least it doesn't if you're not using a formula. Writers everywhere need help building something beautiful, solid, and original, and that takes a method. This is how we do it. This is how it gets done.

You may never have heard of the Book Architecture Method. Or, you may have bought my first book, *Blueprint Your Bestseller: Organize and Revise Any Manuscript with the Book Architecture Method* (hereafter, *BYB*), but didn't look into it too closely because you didn't have enough material to "organize and revise." *BYB* suggests you have at least 60 pages of first-draft material and preferably a hundred before you undertake its 22 action steps. By contrast, you can use the book you are holding now on a manuscript in any stage of completion. Anything you learned from my first book is applicable here, but you don't have to have any prior exposure to jump right in.

The Book Architecture Method uses three main concepts: scene, series, and theme. Let's talk about *scene*. The method says that if you find your 99 scenes, and you put them in the right order, then you will be all set. That's kind of a joke, but I've seen it happen. Please note: 99 is a placeholder because we don't yet know how many scenes your finished manuscript will have: it might have 72, or 138, etc. I am not saying your manuscript must have 99 scenes because to do so would be formulaic. What I am saying is that when we think of our scenes as comprising a certain number, and therefore separate from each other, we can get the flexibility we need to move things around, to discard some and brainstorm others.

I chose the number 99 because it is one short of a hundred. Meaning, we don't achieve *unity*, the ultimate goal of literary creation, by aiming for comprehensiveness. Instead, we have to seek continuity, consistency, and coherence. Don't put everything in, in other words.

It's similar to when you first start learning how to cook and you get "kitchen sink syndrome," as a chef friend of mine calls it. You're making spaghetti sauce and you spy a yellow pepper, so you dice that up and add it. *Chinese five-spice powder?* Sure, let's throw in a dash of that . . . and red wine vinegar . . . and the whole thing ends up tasting kind of like crap. Whereas if you just start with good tomatoes, good olive oil, etc. then you can taste the individual flavors *and* the way they come together. So it is with scene.

Your scenes are where things happen, and because something happened, your scenes are where something changes. Your scenes are where you "show, don't tell," where you use description and dialogue, but they won't be animated at the level of the full-length narrative, unless you use *series*.

What is a series? Let me first tell you what a series is not: it is *not* an interrelated series of books in the same genre that have a lot of the same characters. (It is related to that, but we don't have to worry about that right now.)

Series here is defined as:

> *The repetition and variation of a narrative element so that the repetition and variation creates meaning.*

You may have heard *repetition and variation* applied to art in general: the use of melody in music, the architectural pattern.

Repetition and variation *of a narrative element*—what is that? A narrative element is anything that can be identified in a reader's mind as something discrete, for example, a person, a place, a thing, a relationship or a phrase. In fact, the repetitions and variations of series are how a person becomes a character, how a place becomes a setting, how a thing or object becomes a symbol, how a relationship becomes a dynamic, and how a repeated phrase becomes a key to the philosophy of the work.

Repetition and variation of a narrative element *creates meaning*. It's a little early for that. I promise we will come back to how series creates meaning, and we will see examples of a wide variety of series. In fact, that's all we're really going to talk about.

The repetitions and variations of each series form individual narrative arcs, and we are going to practice graphing these **series arcs**, the first of Book Architecture's three tools. We gain the skills to have these arcs interact, intersect, and collide—to braid these threads of series into a whole tapestry—through the use of **series grids**, the second tool. And we use the third tool of the **series target** to make sure that all of these series are about the same thing, because your book can only be about one thing.

And we call that one thing our *theme*.

Your book can only be about one thing. I say that often enough that one student said, "Your book can only be about one thing—that's *your* one thing." Another student asked, "What about two things? Can my book be about two things?" You know those students. To which I replied, "Yes, provided that those two things are about one thing."

This is as close as I get to a *should*. You should be able to say what the theme of your work is in one sentence. You don't have to worry about whether that one sentence is a cliché. Better to spend your time worrying about whether you believe that one sentence.

"It's not how you fall in life, it's whether you pick yourself up."

Do you believe that? I do. The originality comes from the clothing that you put on the theme, such as:

"How a girl goes from being a drunk crying lesbian to just being a drunk lesbian."

Thank you Jennifer and Brown University for that one. You can feel the change in that, right? She might be all set now. We will see several more examples of theme in the examples that we encounter, such as this one from the novel *Catch-22*:

"Immoral logic seemed to be confounding him at every turn."

When you get your theme, you can place it in the bull's-eye of a series target (our third tool), arrange your series around it, and then use what repeats and varies to drill down to the level of individual scenes to see what your work is still missing, what has to go, and what kind of opportunity you really have in front of you.

Scene, series, and theme. A relatively simple way to think about writing. There are many good books on the market today on the subject of *scene*. My use of *theme* is original in its application but not its definition. *Series,* though, fills a void in the writing world, and it has produced attention, a little controversy, and some a-ha! moments for writers.

There are many different types of series, as I mentioned before. There is a character series: when a person repeats and varies, they become a character; an object series: when an object repeats and varies, it becomes a symbol; a phrase series: when a phrase is repeated, it becomes the message or the mantra of the work; a relationship series: when two or more individuals evolve a dynamic; and a location series: when different scenes take place in the same locale, adding extra significance to it—to name a few of the major ones. There is, of course, an event series as well, but here we have to be careful because if we're not, we'll end up privileging these events above all of the other aspects of the work. We'll call the events a *plot* and make everything else take a backseat.

When I work with writers, they all want to talk with me about their plot. "What is this plot you speak of?" I ask, and they say something like, ". . . you know, everything that happens . . . the important parts . . . the stuff that comes together, and you know, means something."

One word can do all that? Plot used in that way is singular. Does that then mean it is either working or not working? I have found that working with individual series gives us a more productive perspective on how things are unfolding in any narrative. If you want to call them subplots, or narrative arcs, that's fine, just as long as you don't go looking for *the* plot or *the* narrative arc, because you won't find one. Every series contributes to the overall movement and impact of a work, and, as you'll see below, it is instructive to group the building blocks of meaning this way.

When we talk about plot as separate from the characters, the symbols, the locales, the dialogue, and the philosophical introspection, what we are doing is privileging events over everything else. But nothing exists in a vacuum; let's make everything a series instead and immerse ourselves in the continuities, the correspondences, and the cohesion of a narrative that can become our universe.

Writing guides that treat everything separately make returning to unity that much harder. I don't want to sound like one of those people who think they've found the answer while everybody else is wrong. I just feel that current approaches to writing structure will inevitably box you in.

Nowhere is this more true than for the subject of plot. Everybody says pretty much the exact same thing. There is a "universal story" that we all must adhere to: narrative should be divided into a "three-act" structure of conflict, crisis, and resolution. Within these three acts, there are more specific landmarks such as the first "pinch point," where we are reminded of the antagonistic force, or the "midpoint," where we get a twist that sends the main character into a new world.

The whole of it looks more or less like this:

INTRODUCTION:
THE FORMULA

At...

5% **THE OPENING INCIDENT** A DISTURBANCE WHICH HOOKS

10% **THE BEGINNING** SETTING UP THE STAKES

20% **THE END OF THE BEGINNING** PIVOTAL MOMENT WITH ONLY TWO CHOICES

25% **THE POINT OF NO RETURN** THAT CHOICE HAS BEEN MADE

50% **THE MIDPOINT** HERO TAKES CONTROL OF HIS/HER DESTINY

75% **THE CRISIS** GREATEST STRUGGLE SO FAR

80% **THE END** PREPARATION FOR FINAL STEPS

90% **THE CLIMACTIC INCIDENT** ONE FINAL CLASH

95% **THE RESOLUTION** WRAPPING IT UP

...percentage of the story

This is good stuff to think about, just as long as we don't all use it at the same time and create a bunch of narratives that resemble each other because, you know, we all used the same formula. A lot of great books use this formula, but a lot of great books don't. Or, to put it another way: There may be a pre-existing structure in our human psyches that influences how we receive narrative. But we don't start with a formula to get to that structure. We use a method to uncover how you may be working with that structure. (And some people say, "Oh! Wait . . . I was looking for a formula. I'm going to have to call you back!")

Because we have our series, we don't need a formula. By tracking our series, we can straighten out 99 percent of what is wrong with our work. I'm serious; that figure is probably low. You can use the tool of the series arc to ensure consistency with your various throughlines, become aware of any gaping holes, and create moments of emotional impact. You can use the tool of the series grid to time the appearances and interactions of the most important narrative elements to engender dramatic tension and complex emotional and philosophical effects. You can use the tool of the series target to contain the universe of your narrative and give your readers the very comforting feeling that "everything is coming together."

Convinced yet? You don't have to be. All you have to do is give me the benefit of the doubt. Writers just like you swear that the Book Architecture Method has helped them figure out the real story they'd been trying to write. With this method in mind, their experiences of both reading and writing have been totally transformed—the series now jump out like secret codes!

And in case you were out there thinking that famous writers don't have to go through the same processes as the rest of us, because they're geniuses and stuff, let me introduce you to the theme of this book: Intelligent planning is not the enemy of creative genius. John Steinbeck, back me up: "I don't know why writers are never given credit for knowing their craft. Years after I have finished a book, someone discovers my design and ascribes it either to a theft or an accident."[*]

Well, we won't do that. Yes, we will be "discovering the design" of several works in this book, but we will give those writers all the credit. Just as we will give you all the credit when your work comes before the world.

The works that we will be enjoying while we wrap our minds around how to plot and outline without using a formula are as follows:

> "Corduroy" by Don Freeman (children's story)
> *The Great Gatsby* by F. Scott Fitzgerald (novel)
> *Slumdog Millionaire* screenplay by Simon Beaufoy (film)
> *The Social Network* screenplay by Aaron Sorkin (film)
> *Harry Potter and the Order of the Phoenix* by J. K.
>   Rowling (novel)
> *Catch-22* by Joseph Heller (novel)
> *The Metamorphosis* by Franz Kafka (novella)

You do not need to be intimately familiar with the example in order to benefit from each chapter. Each narrative referenced will be briefly synopsized, with at least enough content that you can always infer what is going on. Because I know that you are primarily interested in your own work—as you should be—I promise not to waste your valuable writing time.

I'm supposed to warn you that more concentrative study is required than might be expected from a "how to plot and outline" book. But it's not going to be all work. We are also going to dream that we can write better than we thought we could, and then deliver something that is authentic and powerful for our readers. Let's get started.

---

[*] John Steinbeck, *Journal of a Novel: The East of Eden Letters* (New York: Penguin, 1990), 134.

Chapter One

The Basics of Series in the Short Story "Corduroy"

Let's go over the basics of series so that we can begin using the concept immediately. We know from the Introduction that each series has a **type**: it may be a person, an object, a place, a relationship, or a phrase—to name some popular narrative elements—that repeats and varies. Each time a series appears, we call those examples or occurrences **iterations**. We could have called them examples or occurrences, but I like the way "iteration" reminds us of "reiterated." When something is reiterated (such as during an argument), it is never the same because you had to say it twice. In the same way, when an object reappears, it is never the same, because its condition and its context have changed. We give each series a **name**, something that will quickly bring us back into the essence of that series. In addition to type, number of iterations, and a name, we will later describe each series in a **sentence** that shows the repetitions and variations which it undergoes, and identify the **question** that the series asks and eventually answers.

For a book-length narrative, you may benefit from identifying twelve to fifteen to even eighteen series. Because "Corduroy" is a short story, we will only track three series: the *I've Always Wanted* series, the *Missing Button* series, and the *Money* series. We will prepare a series grid for each of them and then a grand series grid that incorporates all of them together. We'll also draw our first series arc. I think that's all you need to know for now. Oh, and the plural of series is series. Sorry about that.

Synopsis of "Corduroy"

Our first example of series comes from the children's book "Corduroy" by Don Freeman. Do you know this book? Great book. We're going to read it right now. Not really. Kind of.

- Corduroy is a bear in a department store.

- Lisa wants Corduroy the bear. Looking straight into Corduroy's bright eyes, she says: "Oh, Mommy! . . . Look! There's the very bear I've always wanted."

- But Mom's not having it. . . . She's spent too much already today. "Besides, he's lost the button to one of his shoulder straps," she points out.

- So Corduroy, that intrepid soul, goes looking for his missing button. When he gets on the escalator, he says: "Could this be a mountain? I think I've always wanted to climb a mountain."

- He gets off the escalator at the next floor and is surrounded by tables and chairs and rows and rows of beds. "This must be a palace!" Corduroy gasps. "I guess I've always wanted to live in a palace."

- He thinks he finds his missing button when he sees one of those buttons on a mattress. "This must be a bed," he says. "I've always wanted to sleep in a bed."

- And then, because Corduroy is the age of our young readers, he knocks over and breaks a floor lamp . . .

- . . . and he gets discovered by the night watchman . . .

- . . . and it looks like his quest will end prematurely as he is taken back to his floor.

- But look, it's Lisa! She's counted the money she's saved in her piggy bank. . . . And her mother says she has enough . . .

- . . . to bring Corduroy home to be her very own bear! . . .

- Next to her girl-size bed there is a little bed that's just the right size for him. "This must be home," Corduroy says. "I know I've always wanted a home."

- Lisa sews his button back on—not because she doesn't love him just the way he is, but because he'll be more comfortable with his shoulder strap fastened.

- "You must be a friend," Corduroy says. "I've always wanted a friend."

Iterations of the *I've Always Wanted* Series

When we start trying to find our series, all we have to remember is repetition and variation. What do we find repeated? The first series in "Corduroy" that jumps out at us is the *I've Always Wanted* series.

The *I've Always Wanted* series isn't just how my eight-year-old follows along in the story; it helps all of us.

Below is our first series grid, one of the three tools we will be using. Every time I say "series grid," you can think "outline" in your mind—and then toss that word out the window (for reasons we will get into later). This is a pretty simple series grid, so if it looks like something you filled out in junior high when you were "reading for ideas," don't worry—they will grow increasingly complex as our work continues.

CORDUROY:

SERIES GRID 1

ITERATION NUMBER	PAGE NUMBER	SERIES NAME: I'VE ALWAYS WANTED SERIES TYPE: PHRASE
1	3	"OH, MOMMY!" SHE SAID. "LOOK! THERE'S THE VERY BEAR I'VE ALWAYS WANTED."
2	9	"I THINK I'VE ALWAYS WANTED TO CLIMB A MOUNTAIN."
3	11	"THIS MUST BE A PALACE!" CORDUROY GASPED. "I GUESS I'VE ALWAYS WANTED TO LIVE IN A PALACE."
4	12	"THIS MUST BE A BED," HE SAYS, "I'VE ALWAYS WANTED TO SLEEP IN A BED."
5	26	"THIS MUST BE HOME," CORDUROY SAYS. "I KNOW I'VE ALWAYS WANTED A HOME."
6	28	"YOU MUST BE A FRIEND," CORDUROY SAYS. "I'VE ALWAYS WANTED A FRIEND."

Setting up a series grid is easy. In the first column you list the iteration number. After that, you can list the scene name, or the chapter where the iteration appears, or the page number where you find the example in the text. Anyone familiar with *BYB* will know that I made a big deal in that book about finding your individual scenes and slicing them apart from each other. We named our scenes and kept track of them all on a list, adding some and deleting others as the process of revision progressed.* If your manuscript is already in scenes, then by all means use the scene name as your way of indicating where an iteration comes from. In the case of "Corduroy," I have just used the page number where the iteration occurs.

Let's recall the definition of *series*: the repetition and variation of a narrative element so that the repetition and variation creates meaning. If we read the *I've Always Wanted* series closely, we see that we go from "I *think* I've always wanted to climb a mountain" and "I *guess* I've always wanted to live in a palace" to "I *know* I've always wanted a home . . . and a friend" (italics mine). The repetitions and variations create meaning; if we had to define the theme of "Corduroy" based on the direction of this series, I guess we could say that it's an antimaterialist screed about what's really important in this life.

The *Missing Button* Series: The Central Series

The *I've Always Wanted* series may be the one closest to the theme, but it is not the **central series**. The central series, which we will look at more closely in Chapters Three and Four, is the series that lets the reader know where she or he stands; it gives the clearest sense of negotiating time and space. The central series also lets us know what is at stake, what the goal of the story is. This is where we might get back into traditional notions of plot for a bit. You know those people who say there are only a certain number of kinds of plots: quest, revenge, temptation, forbidden love, etc?† We call that the *master plot*

---

* For an extended look at this process, see Chapter One of *Blueprint Your Bestseller,* "What Is a Scene?"

† Ronald B. Tobias, *20 Master Plots: And How to Build Them* (Cincinnati: Writer's Digest Books, 1993).

theory. It might hold true here, kind of, insofar that the master plot describes the central series and not the entire book.

CORDUROY:
SERIES GRID 2

ITERATION NUMBER	PAGE NUMBER	SERIES NAME: MISSING BUTTON SERIES TYPE: OBJECT
1	3	CORDUROY THE BEAR IS MISSING A BUTTON TO ONE OF HIS SHOULDER STRAPS; LISA'S MOTHER THINKS THIS IS A REASON NOT TO BUY CORDUROY, BUT LISA DISAGREES.
2	5	CORDUROY GOES IN SEARCH OF HIS MISSING BUTTON.
3	13	CORDUROY THINKS HE FINDS HIS MISSING BUTTON WHEN HE SEES ONE OF THE BUTTONS ON A MATTRESS.
4	27	LISA SEWS A BUTTON BACK ONTO CORDUROY'S OVERALLS.

According to the master plotters, "Corduroy" is a quest. The *Missing Button* series defines the nature of the quest (Corduroy doesn't have a button), it initiates the action (Corduroy goes looking for his button), it precipitates the turning point (Corduroy tries to pull a button off a mattress, slips, breaks the lamp, thereby alerting the guard, who returns him to his floor), and signals the ending (Lisa sews a button back onto his overalls while speaking about unconditional love).

All of this is true, of course, but these events are not the only things going on in this story. Just tracking the "plot" wouldn't give us a sense of the richness of innocent relationships, which is the effect the narration has on us. As I mentioned at the opening of this chapter, every series has to ask a question. Some of them ask specific questions, such as: Will Corduroy find his missing button? Some are a little more abstract, such as: What has Corduroy really always wanted? Or, in the case of the next series, the *Money* series: What does it mean to be responsible?

How Many Iterations Should I Have? The *Money* Series

After reviewing the two previous series grids shown, you can see how a series with six iterations has a slightly different rhythm than a series with four iterations. You may be wondering how many iterations your series should have.

You have to have at least two. A series with only one iteration will never go anywhere. It won't even register enough to catch our interest. But two iterations can work because the first one establishes the series' identity, and the second one represents its change.

The *Money* series in "Corduroy" is a great example of a two-iteration series.

CORDUROY:
SERIES GRID 3

ITERATION NUMBER	PAGE NUMBER	SERIES NAME: MONEY SERIES TYPE: OBJECT/CONCEPT
1	3	LISA'S MOM HAS SPENT TOO MUCH MONEY ON HER SHOPPING TRIP TO AFFORD TO BUY CORDUROY THE BEAR.
2	23	LISA HAS ENOUGH MONEY SAVED IN HER PIGGY BANK TO BUY CORDUROY THE BEAR.

These two iterations show the difference between spending—"I've spent too much already"—and saving—"Last night I counted what I've saved in my piggy bank and my mother said I could bring you home." Sort of a "God bless the child/who's got his own" thing.

It may only appear twice, but it makes all the difference in the world, influencing the relationship between Lisa and Corduroy more than anything else that happens—her thrift is the reason why his quest ends favorably.

As long as something changes, it can be a series. Remember: repetition *and* variation. In the *I've Always Wanted* series, it is a phrase that repeats and varies, leading us to the theme of the work. In the *Missing Button* series, it is an object which, as it repeats and varies, becomes a symbol, simultaneously generating the central series. In the *Money* series, it is also an object which repeats and varies (even though money is actually both an object and a concept, the coin of the realm).

The repetitions let us know what we are talking about, while the variations give us the direction: things are getting better (improvement), or things are getting worse (deterioration). When something changes, you can plot the narrative arc of that series, what we will be calling the series arc, the second of our three tools. I'm okay with using the word *plot* as a verb so long as we don't refer to the plot as if it were one thing and privilege it above all of the other narrative elements.

On the next page is the simplest series arc there can be, showing the two iterations of the *Money* series. The two iterations span virtually the entire book: of 28 pages, they appear on p. 3 and p. 23. The change is also pretty simple: no money, no Corduroy; money, Corduroy. It is so simple, in fact, that this isn't even really an arc— more of just a line. You need three points on a line to make an arc.

These arcs will get progressively fancier as we go forward, but their rationale remains the same. You can always make an arc of one of your series by grabbing some graph paper and producing an x-axis (horizontal), which spreads the narrative out from the beginning to the end, and labeling the y-axis (vertical) from DETERIORA-TION to IMPROVEMENT. Finding where you want to plot an iteration horizontally is pretty easy: you just find the place in the story where it exists. Finding where you want to plot the iteration vertically is really more of an art than a science. It helps to have all of the iterations

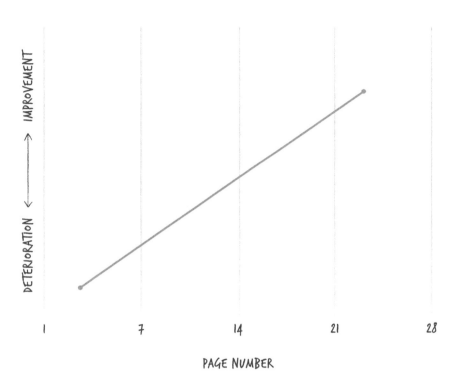

gathered together before you make your series arc; then you can feel the differences in emotion and consequence of each in relation to the others. The truth is, if you use your intuition, you'll be fine, as we will see later when we discuss what value graphing the series arc can bring to your storytelling.

The Key Scene in "Corduroy"

So far we have developed three series grids from the same short story, one for each series. What happens when we put them all together?

In the Book Architecture Method, a *key scene* is defined as a scene where a number of series come together. Having your series interact, intersect, and collide in a scene is what delivers the emotional impact, what pushes the action in a scene past the point of no return. It is what makes your book feel like it would not be your book without it.

If we were to pick a scene from "Corduroy" without which the story wouldn't be the same, we might choose the scene where Lisa asks for Corduroy but is turned down by her mother:

> Then one morning a little girl stopped and looked straight into Corduroy's bright eyes.
>
> "Oh, Mommy!" she said. "Look! There's the very bear I've always wanted."
>
> "Not today, dear." Her mother sighed. "I've spent too much already. Besides, he doesn't look new. He's lost the button to one of his shoulder straps."   (p. 3)

Doesn't it feel like there is a lot going on here? That's because each of the series we have been tracking has an iteration on the very same page. We can see this by introducing different font styles into the same paragraph, so that the text looks like this:

> Then one morning a little girl stopped and looked straight into Corduroy's bright eyes.
>
> "Oh, Mommy!" she said. "Look! There's the very bear *I've always wanted.*"
>
> "Not today, dear." Her mother sighed. "**I've spent too much** already. Besides, he doesn't look new. He's LOST THE BUTTON to one of his shoulder straps."

KEY:
italicized text:	the I've Always Wanted series
bolded text:	the Money series
capitalized text:	the Missing Button series

We can also look at this key scene from the perspective of our first expanded series grid. When we put the three series we have been studying together and highlight the key scene in blue, it looks like this:

CORDUROY:

SERIES GRID 4

PAGE NUMBER	SERIES: I'VE ALWAYS WANTED	SERIES: MISSING BUTTON	SERIES: MONEY
3	THEN ONE MORNING A LITTLE GIRL STOPPED AND LOOKED STRAIGHT INTO CORDUROY'S BRIGHT EYES. "OH, MOMMY!" SHE SAID. "LOOK! THERE'S THE VERY BEAR I'VE ALWAYS WANTED."	CORDUROY THE BEAR IS MISSING A BUTTON TO ONE OF HIS SHOULDER STRAPS; LISA'S MOTHER THINKS THIS IS A REASON NOT TO BUY CORDUROY, BUT LISA DISAGREES.	LISA'S MOM HAS SPENT TOO MUCH MONEY ON HER SHOPPING TRIP TO AFFORD TO BUY CORDUROY THE BEAR.
5		CORDUROY GOES IN SEARCH OF HIS MISSING BUTTON.	
9	"I THINK I'VE ALWAYS WANTED TO CLIMB A MOUNTAIN."		
11	"THIS MUST BE A PALACE!" CORDUROY GASPED. "I GUESS I'VE ALWAYS WANTED TO LIVE IN A PALACE."		
12	"THIS MUST BE A BED," HE SAYS, "I'VE ALWAYS WANTED TO SLEEP IN A BED."		
13		CORDUROY THINKS HE FINDS HIS MISSING BUTTON WHEN HE SEES ONE OF THE BUTTONS ON A MATTRESS.	
23			LISA HAS ENOUGH MONEY SAVED IN HER PIGGY BANK TO BE ABLE TO BUY CORDUROY THE BEAR.
26	"THIS MUST BE HOME," CORDUROY SAYS. "I KNOW I'VE ALWAYS WANTED A HOME.		
27	LISA SEWS A BUTTON BACK ON CORDUROY'S OVERALLS.		
28	"YOU MUST BE A FRIEND," CORDUROY SAYS. "I'VE ALWAYS WANTED A FRIEND."		

In subsequent chapters, we'll look at how series iterations are staggered to produce the effects of foreshadowing and suspense. Let's pause here, however, to reflect on your own work.

Getting Hands-on:

While you were reading this chapter, did certain series from your work come to mind? Are there repetitions in your work that might hold the key to the meaning you are trying to convey? You can start a list of your series now with the basic elements of each: its name, its type, and its number of iterations. If you are in doubt about the value or extent of a particular series, put it on the list for now. You can always drop some series from the list (and from your book!) later.

Chapter Two

Using Series to Build Character in F. Scott Fitzgerald's *The Great Gatsby*

In the previous chapter, we saw that a series has five components.

A series has a **name**

A series has a **type**

A series has a certain number of **iterations**

The repetitions and variations of a series can be described in a **sentence** that indicates the changes it goes through

A series asks—and eventually answers—a **question**

This chapter will focus primarily on the second of these components, the series type, and specifically on the type of series represented by characters (character series). For our example, we will use the novel *The Great Gatsby* by F. Scott Fitzgerald. You probably don't need me to synopsize *Gatsby* for you. I mean, who hasn't read it, besides me up until a couple of years ago? I came away feeling like it was the best novel I have ever read. And you know, I'm supposed to know about stuff like this.

I could probably write this entire book using *Gatsby* as the only example. That's what Gérard Genette did in his book *Narrative Discourse*—he just used Marcel Proust's *Remembrance of Things Past*, and that was it. I'm a little rusty on my Proust and, besides, it's more than a thousand pages. *Gatsby*'s only 180 pages in my version*—all the more impressive, in my opinion, to get all of this done. The more you study it, the more it just keeps getting better. I will remain true to the endeavor here and tell you what you need to know to set up a specific example, but this chapter will not tell you everything you need to know about *The Great Gatsby*. Hopefully, though, it will tell you a lot of what you need to know about using series to reveal character.

Foreshadowing in *The Great Gatsby*

Let's start small. F. Scott Fitzgerald was a master of foreshadowing. At the end of the previous chapter, I promised that series would help you with your foreshadowing. You have likely heard this term while being treated to vague definitions of it. In the context of series, it gets much clearer: foreshadowing is the first iteration in a series. It establishes the existence of a series in the narrative often in an indirect way that merely plants a seed in the reader's mind. *How* indirect is often the measure of a writer's skill in terms of how far spaced out the iterations are while still being memorable. Besides the stuff you *have* to make obvious and the stuff you *want* to make obvious, there is material that exists in the periphery of the reader's mind, and when you use it again, it has the effect that you really know what you're doing. Foreshadowing draws the outlines of a world that the reader then colors in.

---

* I am using the seemingly standard Scribner paperback edition, first published in 2004 (New York).

Check this out:

THE GREAT GATSBY:
SERIES GRID

ITERATION NUMBER	PAGE NUMBER	SERIES NAME: WHO HAS AN INNOCENT HEART (AND WE WANT TO SEE END UP TOGETHER) SERIES TYPE: CHARACTER
1	9	(DAISY) LAUGHED AGAIN, AS IF SHE SAID SOMETHING VERY WITTY, AND HELD MY HAND FOR A MOMENT, LOOKING UP INTO MY FACE, PROMISING THAT THERE WAS NO ONE IN THE WORLD SHE SO MUCH WANTED TO SEE. THAT WAS A WAY SHE HAD.
2	48	(GATSBY) SMILED UNDERSTANDINGLY—MUCH MORE THAN UNDERSTANDINGLY. IT WAS ONE OF THOSE RARE SMILES WITH A QUALITY OF ETERNAL REASSURANCE IN IT, THAT YOU MAY COME ACROSS FOUR OR FIVE TIMES IN LIFE. IT FACED—OR SEEMED TO FACE—THE WHOLE EXTERNAL WORLD FOR AN INSTANT, AND THEN CONCENTRATED ON YOU WITH AN IRRESISTIBLE PREJUDICE IN YOUR FAVOR.

One of these iterations foreshadows the other; we can call it the *Who Has an Innocent Heart (and We Want to See End Up Together)* series. There are only two iterations in this series, which, you may remember, is the minimum number we need to make a series. In this case, not only is it all we need, it's all we want. Fitzgerald wants to link Daisy, the helpless, newly married debutante with Jay Gatsby, the mysterious millionaire—and only those two. I think it's perfectly fine, by the way, to ask what the author was trying to do. Because he's doing it anyway so we might as well try to see how.

Foreshadowing doesn't have to be used just to develop character, of course. Fitzgerald uses it for everything from objects, like billboards and swimming pools, to the most impactful events, such as when our narrator, the humble bond salesman Nick Carraway, finds out that it was Daisy and not Gatsby who had been driving the car that struck and killed Myrtle Wilson.

A bigger moment the book doesn't know. Yet it is foreshadowed by a totally separate, and seemingly harmless escapade, that involves none of the main characters. At Gatsby's lavish party ninety pages earlier, the drunken booklover Owl Eyes has no explanation for why the car in which he was traveling went into a ditch. When he tries to explain the accident to other partygoers, he stumbles when attempting to convey the information that someone else was driving:

> "But how did it happen? Did you run into the wall?"
>
> "Don't ask me," said Owl Eyes, washing his hands of the whole matter. "I know very little about driving—next to nothing. It happened, and that's all I know."
>
> "Well, if you're a poor driver you oughtn't to try driving at night."
>
> "But I wasn't even trying," he explained indignantly, "I wasn't even trying."
>
> An awed hush fell upon the bystanders.
>
> "Do you want to commit suicide? . . ."
>
> "You don't understand," explained the criminal. "I wasn't driving. There's another man in the car."   (p. 54)

This is an event series with two iterations. The same "Ah-h-h!" that ripples through the crowd in the first iteration echoes in our minds, and whether or not we can consciously recall this event in the second and last iteration, when we find out that Gatsby is not responsible for vehicular manslaughter, it is there somewhere.

Series Sentences in *The Great Gatsby*

If you completed the "Getting Hands-on" section at the end of the last chapter, you have started a list of your series. When we are doing series work, we start with the name, type, and number of iterations. Chasing down all of the iterations can be some work, but it is quite beneficial when the time comes to analyze what is missing from your manuscript or what you have in excess. When you have collected all of your iterations, you are in a good place to write out your series sentence: a one-line description of the repetitions and variations that indicate either the tension inherent in the series or the change the series undergoes over the course of the narrative. What makes it interesting and relevant, in other words.

Here are some series sentences from *The Great Gatsby* along with the series name in italics and the series type in parentheses. (Note: Some of these are more than one sentence, but I am taking the opportunity to also synopsize the narrative element presented.)

- *West Egg vs. East Egg* (location): These two Long Island communities are pitched against each other, with the first being the "less fashionable" and full of "crazy fish" versus the second, which may be more fashionable but "chafed under (its) old euphemisms."

- *Nick's Poverty* (character): Our main character sells bonds, so how bad can it be? However, he says he's too poor to marry, is afraid people will "know" and "disapprove" of him, and has to pick up a woman's pocketbook that has been dropped on the train "by the extreme tip of the corners to indicate that I had no designs upon it—but every one [. . .] suspected me just the same."   (p. 115)

- *The Green Light* (object): Probably the most celebrated series in the book; Gatsby has been pursuing Daisy for five years until finally moving into a mansion across the bay from her, and thereby potentially becoming her social equal and winning her hand. Gatsby stretches his arms and can almost reach the green light at the end of Daisy's dock. He fails to achieve his goal, but he goes to his death still believing in "the green light."

- *The Past* (concept): Nick and Gatsby differ philosophically about whether one can repeat the past. Gatsby is banking on it: "I'm going to fix everything just the way it was before," he said, nodding determinedly. "She'll see." (p. 110)

- *Gatsby's Swimming Pool* (object): Gatsby hasn't "made use of it all summer" (p. 82); he stops the gardener from draining the pool because "I've never used that pool all summer" (p. 153); then he ends up floating in it after being shot dead by Wilson, the garage mechanic, in a case of mistaken revenge. (p. 162)

Gatsby's Swimming Pool is a classic three-iteration series; in fact, three is the magic number for a series. I often give the advice: If you got it once, use it twice (in order to register it as a series in the reader's mind). Three times is a charm.

When we look at the five series presented above, we can see they represent a wide variety of series type. What do we have so far? A pair of dueling locales, a social condition, a concept (involving the memory and action), and two objects. In this chapter, we will also be looking at the *T. J. Eckleburg* billboard (another object), the colloquialism *"Old Sport"* (phrase), as well as several series that reveal both the similarities and the differences in character. My point is that what can repeat and vary is far more than just a catalogue of events, and a breadth of series types adds to the overall texture of the narrative in a unique and irreplaceable way.

How "Show, Don't Tell" Really Works

"Show, don't tell" is often the first and most compelling piece of writing advice we hear. Yet most of us think of this principle as only happening inside a particular scene: we get characters to say things as opposed to think things; we describe a character through specific indicators such as their dress, physique, and speech.

A scene can do a lot of wonderful things. In *BYB*, I gave five definitions of scene. The first two I offered were: 1) *A scene is where something happens;* and 2) *A scene is where, because something happens, something changes.** But scenes occupy only one space in time, one "plot," if you will. Later in *BYB*, I offered a third definition: *A scene has to be capable of series.* Larger arcs of the narrative as a whole have to be able to move through a multiple number of scenes. The change that takes place in a scene pushes a particular series in a direction of either improvement or deterioration, but we don't actually get a transformation unless those scenes are part of a series.

Let me show you what I mean. The billboard of the long-retired oculist (optometrist) Doctor *T. J. Eckleburg* presides over the stop on the train line between New York City and West Egg and East Egg. This stop is less a town than a dismal locale where the bleak dust of all the city's ash is retired in heaps. It is a liminal place, and the *T. J. Eckleburg* sign is a symbol of this. As Nick narrates:

> The eyes of Doctor T. J. Eckleburg are blue and gigantic—their retinas are one yard high. They look out of no face, but, instead, from a pair of enormous yellow spectacles which pass over a non-existent

---

*   For all five definitions of scene, see *Blueprint Your Bestseller,* p. 35, 118, and 133.

nose. Evidently some wild wag of an oculist set them there to fatten his practice in the borough of Queens, and then sank down himself into eternal blindness, or forgot them and moved away. But his eyes, dimmed a little by many paintless days under sun and rain, brood on over the solemn dumping ground. (p. 24)

What do you take away from this at first read? "Many paintless days . . ." This sign is fading over a land that prosperity forgot. This is "Show, don't tell" at the level of the scene. But nothing is moving into action, until the next iteration of the *T. J. Eckleburg* series, when Nick; Tom, Daisy's husband; and Jordan, Nick's erstwhile girlfriend, stop for gas on their ride to the city. Nick sees:

Over the ashheaps the giant eyes of Doctor T. J. Eckleburg kept their vigil but I perceived, after a moment, that other eyes were regarding us with peculiar intensity from less than twenty feet away. (p. 124)

Can these eyes see? Every series has to ask a question. Another seed is planted, even as we realize that no, the eyes belong to Myrtle, Tom's mistress, who has gone terrified with jealousy as she stares down at Jordan, whom she guesses incorrectly to be Tom's wife. This is iteration #2 of three—three is the magic number, after all.

In the climax of the *T. J. Eckleburg* series, the billboard's perceptual ability is made fully evident. The garage attendant, Wilson, has confirmed for himself that his wife, Myrtle, has been cheating on him with someone whom he doesn't yet know:

"I spoke to her," he muttered, after a long silence. "I told her she might fool me but she couldn't fool God. I took her to the window"—with an effort he got up and walked to the rear window and leaned with his face pressed against it—"and I said 'God knows what you've been doing, everything you've been doing. You may fool me, but you can't fool God!'"

Standing behind him, Michaelis saw with a shock that he was looking at the eyes of Doctor T. J. Eckleburg, which had just emerged, pale and enormous, from the dissolving night.

"God sees everything," repeated Wilson.

"That's an advertisement," Michaelis assured him. (p. 159–60)

Fitzgerald cracks me up. Beyond that, this is the way a great fictional narrative works, presenting us with different sides of the same question without ever quite giving an answer. This is what "Show, don't tell" is really driving at. We show as opposed to tell so that everybody can make up his or her mind, which gets more important, the more important the stakes. As an object series, the *T. J. Eckleburg* sign becomes a proxy for nothing short of a character's religious understanding: Nick is agnostic, Wilson is the devout believer, Michaelis, the coffee shop owner, is a disbelieving pragmatist. One scene alone can't create this complex effect without simply devolving into a debate between talking heads. But a series that emerges over time doesn't have to tell us anything. Now we're being shown something!

Series Create Our Complex Understanding of Character

In a novel like *Gatsby*, many of the series contribute in some way to our understanding of character. The central series, that overriding question which spans from (nearly) the beginning to (nearly) the end is a series of character identity. I'm calling it *Who Is Gatsby?* This fabulously wealthy party thrower, where did he come from? How did he make his money? Will poking around reveal the truth? And if the truth does get out, what kind of a difference will it make?

Gatsby is what we will refer to as a "round" character, one who evolves throughout the course of the narrative, as opposed to a "flat" character, who doesn't undergo a change. A flat character only needs one series; a round character can benefit from as many series as you can introduce that: a) the reader can remember, and b) you can make interact and intersect in meaningful ways. Multiple series are, in fact, what give a main character enough interior space to allow them to be called round.

Gatsby has several series that belong to him, including:

- *Gatsby's Name* (character): We meet him as Jay Gatsby, but it is eventually revealed that his real name is James Gantz, the son of dirt-poor farmers in North Dakota. As a way of going even further back, when Gatsby's father shows up for his funeral, he asks, "Where have they got Jimmy?"

- *Ill-informed Whispering* (character): Partygoers at Gatsby's mansion are just as clueless as we are at the beginning. Who is Gatsby? "Well, they say he's a nephew or a cousin of Kaiser Wilhelm's. That's where all his money comes from." (p. 32) "Somebody told me they thought he killed a man once." (p. 44) "I don't think it's so much THAT . . . it's more that he was a German spy during the war." (p. 44) This ill-informed whispering will eventually morph into Tom committing to unmask Gatsby as a way of recapturing the affection of his wife, Daisy. "'Who is this Gatsby anyhow?' demanded Tom suddenly. 'Some big bootlegger?' . . . 'I'd like to know who he is and what he does,' insisted Tom. 'And I think I'll make a point of finding out.'" (p. 108)

- *Gatsby's Education* (character): One of the rumors is that Gatsby was an "Oxford man." (p. 49) It is later revealed that Gatsby went to Oxford for only five months as part of "an opportunity they gave to some of the officers after the Armistice." (p. 129)

Each of these character series contributes something specific to that larger question, the central series, *Who Is Gatsby?* One of the most memorable character series we can use to track the discovery of Gatsby's identity is the *Old Sport* series. The repetitions and variations of this series and the way it drives the narrative forward make it a series at its very finest.

After she saw the 2013 film adaptation of *Gatsby* for the first time, my wife left the TV muttering, ". . . that annoyed me, that 'Old Sport.'" She doesn't care much for pretension in real life, either.* Gatsby's affected expression, "Old Sport," is one that he uses to pass himself off as a "man of fine breeding" when he is actually only an "elegant young roughneck." Calling people "Old Sport," along with reading "improving book[s]" and "practice[ing] elocution," is part of Gatsby's lifelong quest to move up the social ladder.

Let's look more closely at the execution of the *Old Sport* series. It asks the question: Is Gatsby actually a man of fine breeding, or is it all an act? It's interesting to note that we encounter the first iteration of this series before we even know it is Gatsby who is speaking. Nick meets a man at Gatsby's party who says he recognizes him from the war:

> We talked for a moment about some wet, gray little villages in France. Evidently he lived in this vicinity, for he told me that he had just bought a hydroplane, and was going to try it out in the morning.

---

* Yet she still calls me that sometimes. I told you it was memorable.

> "Want to go with me, old sport? Just near the
> shore along the Sound."   (p. 47)

This is Gatsby, of course, but the fact that the first iteration is buried links the phrase to our perception of his character indelibly. When Nick finds out, we encounter the second iteration of the *Old Sport* series right away. Gatsby tells him: "I thought you knew, old sport. I'm afraid I'm not a very good host."

I have drawn the *Old Sport* series arc below. Along the x-axis, I have simply spread out the page numbers in the book, not paying special attention to the other ways you can divide a narrative, such as scenes or chapters, for the sake of this example. Along the y-axis

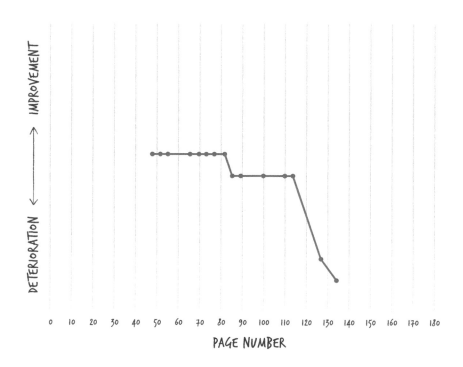

THE GREAT GATSBY:
'OLD SPORT' SERIES ARC

IMPROVEMENT

DETERIORATION

PAGE NUMBER

we have the continuum between IMPROVEMENT and DETERIORATION, which may be by now becoming familiar. For the most part, the first half dozen iterations straddle that line between improvement and deterioration. "Old sport" is just a facet of Gatsby's character that we don't know what to make of, so it appears linear.

The *Old Sport* series arc starts to decline when Nick catches Gatsby forgetting to act in character for a moment:

> [. . .]Together we scrutinized the twelve lemon cakes from the delicatessen shop.
> "Will they do?" I asked.
> "Of course, of course! They're fine!" and he added hollowly, ". . .old sport."   (p. 84)

When Gatsby leaves "his elegant sentences unfinished" and his restlessness "break[s] through his punctilious manner," we wonder, like Nick, about this man whose "elaborate formality of speech just missed being absurd." Nick tries to retain his agnosticism, even as he goes back and forth in his estimation of Gatsby's essential character.

Tom does not have that problem. He sees through Gatsby's pretension, and the *Old Sport* series becomes confrontational. Tom asks Gatsby:

> "All this 'old sport' business. Where'd you pick that up?"
> "Now see here, Tom," said Daisy, turning around from the mirror, "if you're going to make personal remarks I won't stay here a minute."   (p. 127)

Every series worth tracking has to enter the action at some point. Eventually, this scene escalates to a full-scale conflict between Tom and Gatsby, and *Old Sport* is at the heart of it.

"You can suit yourself about that, old sport." said Gatsby steadily.

"I found out what your 'drug stores' were." (Tom) turned to us and spoke rapidly. "He and this Wolfsheim bought up a lot of side-street drug stores here and in Chicago and sold grain alcohol over the counter. That's one of his little stunts. I picked him for a bootlegger the first time I saw him and I wasn't far wrong."

"What about it?" said Gatsby politely. "I guess your friend Walter Chase wasn't too proud to come in on it."

"And you left him in the lurch, didn't you? You let him go to jail for a month over in New Jersey. God! You ought to hear Walter on the subject of *you*."

"He came to us dead broke. He was very glad to pick up some money, old sport."

"Don't you call me 'old sport'!" cried Tom. (p. 134)

This exchange, and Gatsby's violence that follows it, tips the scales in Daisy's eyes irrevocably in Tom's favor, and the *Old Sport* series arc is the pivot that sends the action spiraling downward. We will see that charting individual series arcs can be valuable for many reasons, but none are more valuable than tracing the emotional impact of a sudden sharp rise or decline. A scene may be worth a thousand words, but a series is worth ten thousand.

At this point in the novel, Daisy falls under Tom's control, but oddly enough, we don't. Even though Gatsby may be a criminal and a phony, we see him simply as a man doing what he has to do to follow his dream "right through to the end." The reason that we prefer Gatsby to Tom is because we have been set up to feel this way by earlier series such as the *Rise of the Colored Empires*.

Series Show Us Who to Root For: The *Rise of the Colored Empires* Series

I know it's a little long for a series name, but nothing quite says it any better. We are told Daisy's husband, Tom, has a "simple mind." Remember, this is the guy who is capable of pronouncements such as, "I read somewhere that the sun's getting hotter every year . . . pretty soon the earth's going to fall into the sun—or wait a minute—it's just the opposite—the sun's getting colder every year." (p. 118) But this simplicity is married with distaste when he espouses his philosophy in the *Rise of the Colored Empires* series.

> "Civilization's going to pieces," broke out Tom violently. "I've gotten to be a terrible pessimist about things. Have you read 'The Rise of the Colored Empires' by this man Goddard?"
>
> "Why, no," I answered, rather surprised by his tone.
>
> "Well, it's a fine book, and everybody ought to read it. The idea is if we don't look out the white race will be—will be utterly submerged. It's all scientific stuff; it's been proved." (p. 12–13)

Fitzgerald was exposed to this line of thinking at Princeton by people such as Professor Carl Brigham, who also happened to lead an anti-immigration coalition and helped develop the SAT to keep the riffraff out of the Ivy League. But I digress. The two main female characters don't seem to embrace Tom's fanaticism. In order to get out of trouble with Tom, Daisy claims she was just talking to Nick about "[o]ur white girlhood [which] was passed there. Our beautiful white—" Tom knows he's being spoofed, but he still can't help himself from devolving into racism as a philosophy:

"Self-control!" repeated Tom incredulously. "I suppose the latest thing is to sit back and let Mr. Nobody from Nowhere make love to your wife. Well, if that's the idea you can count me out . . . Nowadays people begin by sneering at family life and family institutions, *and next they'll throw everything overboard and have intermarriage between black and white.*"

Flushed with his impassioned gibberish, he saw himself standing alone on the last barrier of civilization.

"We're all white here," murmured Jordan. (p. 130, italics mine)

Like I said, Fitzgerald cracks me up. This virtual non sequitur shows just how far Tom's view of his membership in the ruling class is removed from America's professed ideals. But the *Rise of the Colored Empires* series takes it one step further by having a counterpoint. Nick is going out to lunch with Gatsby, who is driving. Nick notes:

[t]he city seen from the Queensboro Bridge is always the city seen for the first time, in its first wild promise of all the mystery and the beauty in the world.

[. . .] As we crossed Blackwell's Island a limousine passed us, driven by a white chauffeur, in which sat three modish Negroes, two bucks and a girl. I laughed aloud as the yolks of their eyeballs rolled toward us in haughty rivalry.

"Anything can happen now that we've slid over this bridge," I thought; "anything at all. . . ."

Even Gatsby could happen, without any particular wonder.   (p. 68–69)

Gatsby represents nothing less than the new world order waiting to be born, an apparent meritocracy that nonetheless has to turn to crime to get a foothold. Series—in this case, a philosophy that repeats and varies—reveals character and helps sway us as readers to one side or the other. In this case, probably just one side.

Series Show Us What Characters Have in Common: The *Phone* Series

Fitzgerald, however, doesn't want to make anything too easy. At the same time that we are presented with the dissimilarity between Gatsby and Tom, we are presented with a certain similarity, namely that we don't know what either of these men is really up to. This presents itself to us most clearly through the *Phone* series.

In Tom's case, the *Phone* series is simple, just as he is. Like the *Old Sport* series, Tom's shady side is first revealed by a buried iteration, meaning that it is being talked about but not yet named.

> The butler came back and murmured something close to Tom's ear, whereupon Tom frowned, pushed back his chair, and without a word went inside.   (p. 14)

Where is he going, and why? The answer comes closer to us in the next iteration:

> "Why—" she said hesitantly, "Tom's got some woman in New York."
> "Got some woman?" I repeated blankly.
> Miss Baker nodded.
> "She might have the decency not to telephone him at dinner time. Don't you think?"   (p. 15)

Tom returns to the table, at which point the phone finally rings, "startlingly," as Fitzgerald describes it perfectly tongue-in-cheek. Daisy shakes her head, and Tom does not go pick it up. Nick says:

> "I couldn't guess what Daisy and Tom were thinking, but I doubt if even Miss Baker, who seemed to have mastered a certain hardy scepticism, was able utterly to put this fifth guest's shrill metallic urgency out of mind."   (p. 15)

Tom has been guilty of womanizing in the past, of course, resulting in the kind of careless accidents that the ultrarich seemed to not only be capable of in *Gatsby*, but always escape from scot-free. Daisy chases after Tom at a party, offering him the use of her "little gold pencil" if he wants to take down any addresses. She doesn't really mean it, of course, and whenever Tom's current lover intrudes on the scene, it sets off discomfort that stops all socializing in its tracks.

> "The rumor is," whispered Jordan, "that that's Tom's girl on the telephone."   (p. 116)

Tom uses the phone for illicit sex, while Gatsby uses it for ill-gotten money (we think). Because it is the same symbol, it blends the series of two different characters in a way that implies their similarities more than their differences. Maybe it's simply a case of picking your poison.

When the phone rings for Gatsby, it always seems to be a city on the other end. In fact we could say that *Cities* is a subseries of the *Phone* series: *Cities* are easy to grab on to, after all. Because we are given a little more each time, this is one of those narrative throughlines that gives the reader hope that everything will all make sense in the end.

> Chicago was calling him on the wire.   (p. 48)

> "Philadelphia wants you on the 'phone,
> sir."   (p. 53)
> "Yes . . . Well, I can't talk now . . . I can't talk
> now, old sport . . . I said a *small* town . . . He must
> know what a small town is. . . . Well, he's no use to
> us if Detroit is his idea of a small town . . ."   (p. 93)

It's tempting when we list series this way to consider them as linear, but, in reality, they have more energy than that. Through their variations they can push us into a conclusion that at once we see coming and don't want to believe. Gatsby has been waiting for Daisy's call to let him know that his long unrequited love is finally gliding into shore, but "no telephone message arrived." In the next *Phone* iteration, Nick tries to call Gatsby, but his line is busy.

Uh-oh. In fact, we never see Gatsby again. After his demise, the *Phone* series undergoes another variation, in which Nick is in charge of making Gatsby's funeral preparations and coincidentally answering the phone.

> When the phone rang that afternoon and Long
> Distance said Chicago was calling I thought this
> would be Daisy at last. But the connection came
> through as a man's voice, very thin and far away.
> "This is Slagle speaking . . ."
> "Yes?" The name was unfamiliar.
> "Hell of a note, isn't it? Get my wire?"
> "There haven't been any wires."
> "Young Parke's in trouble," he said rapidly.
> "They picked him up when he handed the bonds
> over the counter. They got a circular from New York
> giving 'em the numbers just five minutes before.
> What d'you know about that, hey? You never can
> tell in these hick towns—"

"Hello!" I interrupted breathlessly. "Look here—
this isn't Mr. Gatsby. Mr. Gatsby's dead."

There was a long silence on the other end of the
wire, followed by an exclamation . . . then a quick
squawk as the connection was broken.   (p. 166–67)

This last iteration contains the *Cities* subseries, along with Gatsby's people shedding some more light on the overarching *Who Is Gatsby?* series—not quite a lot of light, but enough for us to know that however he made his money, it doesn't sound very legal. Ashes to ashes, dust to dust—in series as it is in life; the announcement of Gatsby's death ends the *Phone* series. After that it doesn't ever ring.

It is tempting at this point to construct one giant series grid that shows a hierarchy in which *Who is Gatsby?* appears at the top, with his *Name,* the *Ill-informed Whispering* about him, his *Education,* and his use of the *Phone* underneath that, and the *Cities* who might be calling him under that. But I think we'll hold off on that kind of effort until at least Chapter Five.

For now it's enough that we appreciate the way using series can reveal the complexities of one character as well as the complex relationship between characters. This work is done by presenting series that are clear in their own right. Remember, a complex book does not come from complex series that are difficult to navigate; that's called confusion. Complexity comes from clear, meaningful series that intersect and interact in unusual and consequential ways. It is the blending of these series and these characters that produces a unifying effect, which is what we look for in books. Otherwise we could just go wander outside into the street and encounter all the chaos we might ever need. What we want to see instead is *e pluribus unum*: from many, one.

Getting Hands-on:

You can now expand your list of series, either by adding new series to the list or fleshing out those already present, with their *type,* their *number of iterations,* a *sentence* that describes the change or tension that their repetition and variation indicates, and the *question* that the series asks. Pay special attention to the series that are aspects of a round character. Do these series speak to each other, thereby building up an overall picture of a person?

Chapter Three

Use of the Central Series in *Slumdog Millionaire,* screenplay by Simon Beaufoy

I n the first two chapters, we have seen several examples of what constitutes a series. We have seen how a series helps create characters, deploy objects, inhabit places, arrange allegiances and conflicts, and communicate the theme. These functions benefit the narrative by adding texture, meaning, and coherence—all of which will make your book great. But what about the action, those events that drive the narrative forward? Is that a series as well, or do we have to resort to calling everything else a series but that device a . . . plot?

Fear not. In this book, everything will be considered a series, including the chain of events that answers the most basic question of the story. We call this most basic series the **central series**, and it spans nearly the length of the narrative. We saw it in "Corduroy": Will the teddy bear find his *Missing Button*? We saw it in *The Great Gatsby* with the *Who is Gatsby?* series.

The central series signals that something has begun—a quest in the case of Corduroy, a mystery in the case of Gatsby. With a central series like these, we always know where we stand—whether we are somewhere in the middle, or we are approaching the end. The central series provides the focal point for readers to return to; it's our home base. This is why a central series can help us when we are using multiple timelines—and, by multiple timelines, I also mean flashbacks, so don't tune me out just yet if you're thinking you just want to tell a simple story and are not planning to create a multilayered narrative.

When we go about looking for our central series, it is useful to bear these three things in mind:

- *The central series is the easiest to track.*

- *The central series asks the most basic question.*

- *The central series returns us to the present timeline.*

The Central Series in *Slumdog Millionaire:* The *Q & A* Series

To illustrate the potential of a great central series, I will turn to the film *Slumdog Millionaire*, which won the Academy Award for Best Screenplay in 2008. Not that that means anything necessarily, but it is a fine example of craft. In this film, Jamal, a young man from the lowest caste in India, who lives in the slums and works a menial job transporting tea to workers at a telemarketing center, ends up on the Indian version of the television game show *Who Wants to Be a Millionaire?* Despite Jamal's obvious lack of education and unsophisticated and simpleminded demeanor, he has answered every question right so far, leading him to the final question, good for 20 million rupees.[*]

At that point, he is arrested and subjected to an abusive interrogation: everyone thinks he has cheated—how else could he have

---

[*] About half a million dollars in the year the film came out.

known all of the answers so far? Jamal is forced to recount to the police inspector his diverse and often tragic life experiences that led him to his peculiar knowledge base.

This begins the central series of the film: the progression of questions Jamal is asked during the quiz show, what we will call the *Q & A* series. It fits each of the definitions we have already introduced and now will turn to in a little more detail.

The central series is the easiest to track.

In *Slumdog Millionaire*, the ten iterations of the *Q & A* series correspond to the increasing value of the question asked. They go in chronological order, which helps us keep track, and they are also

SLUMDOG MILLIONAIRE:
SERIES GRID

ITERATION NUMBER	SCENE NUMBER	SERIES NAME: Q & A SERIES TYPE: CENTRAL
1	18	1,000 RUPEES
2	26	4,000 RUPEES
3	30	16,000 RUPEES
4	40	64,000 RUPEES
5	48	250,000 RUPEES
6	85	1 MILLION RUPEES
7	112	2.5 MILLION RUPEES
8	123	5 MILLION RUPEES
9	128	10 MILLION RUPEES
10	177	20 MILLION RUPEES

fairly evenly spaced out, as you can see from the scene number of the movie (out of 197) where the iteration appears, so we never forget about the central series.

The central series asks the most basic question.

You will recall that every series should ask a question; there should always be something at stake. As the playwriting theorist Louis Catron once said, when the questions are answered, the play is over. Using your series can help you figure out how you can have more than one thing at stake at a time, but the central series is the most obvious thing at stake. A strong central series presents a question that should require most of the narrative to answer. In this case, will Jamal answer all of the trivia questions correctly? Or will he get one wrong and lose everything? Or will he drop out, take the money, and run? Vikas Swarup, the author of the novel that *Slumdog Millionaire* was based on, thought the *Q & A* series was important enough that he titled his novel *Q & A*. (Often you can get your title from the theme of your book, but sometimes a series can work just as well.)

The central series returns us to the present timeline.

There are actually three timelines in *Slumdog Millionaire*: the quiz show's questions and answers (*Q & A*); scenes from Jamal's child-hood, which explain how he got the answers; and the timeline of the interrogation, which takes place between questions #9 and #10.

Something I have often noticed is that, when confronted with multiple timelines, we tend to choose one and equate it to our present while we are reading a book or watching a film. I don't know why we do this; I don't have all the answers! Call it narrative behavior. Just know that your audience needs exactly one timeline set in the present. We might call this timeline the "reading present" or the "viewing present."

Once we are thoroughly anchored to the present timeline of the quiz show, the film is able to cut to the scenes from Jamal's life that help explain how he got each answer, all without losing the audience. "Who was the star of the 1973 hit film *Zanjeer*?" A: Amitabh Bacchan; Jamal got his autograph once when the famous actor visited the slum decades ago. "Who wrote the famous song 'Chalo Ri Murali'?" Jamal knows the answer because for a time he was held by a local crime lord who forced his captives to sing this song in the streets for money.

Because it returns us to the present timeline, the central series, in this case the *Q&A* series, is what makes flashbacks possible. Because it is easy to track, the central series helps us become accustomed to the movement from the present to the past and back again, and this movement is benefitted by following some basic rules. In *BYB*, I listed four rules for using flashbacks:

1. When we flash back, we do so for a reason, which is revealed to the reader/viewer eventually.

2. We don't leave the present for so long that the reader/viewer loses his or her bearings upon return.

3. We don't flash back for too short a time.

4. Information in the past is contained in scene, with all of the benefits a scene creates: immediacy, reality, and suspense.

The flashbacks in *Slumdog Millionaire* accomplish all of these guidelines.

Narrative Order versus Chronological Order

If you are working on a manuscript, you can use the three criteria presented above to choose your central series. Pick one that is easy to track, asks a basic question, and establishes the present timeline of your work. One question you will want to consider with any series is whether you put the iterations in chronological order (the order in which they happened) or in narrative order (a different order than when they happened, rearranged for additional emphasis). When working with multiple timelines, I always recommend putting each individual timeline in chronological order.

Although *Slumdog Millionaire* jumps around over nearly two decades, each of the three timelines we reviewed is in chronological order. The quiz show proceeds sequentially from 1,000 rupees to 20 million rupees. Jamal's past spans from the age of five to his early twenties. The interrogation goes from the evening of one day through to the evening of the next day. As I said in the last chapter, a complex book does not come from complex series that are difficult to navigate; that's called confusion. Complexity comes from clear, meaningful series that intersect and interact in unusual and consequential ways.

If you are not using multiple timelines but *do* want to use flashbacks, the principle of the central series still applies. Your flashbacks may be from all over the place, but, if you have a strong central series, the reader will always find his way back to the present action.

The Central Series is Still a Series

Like all good series, the *Q & A* series operates through repetitions and variations—first the repetitions, then the variations. First, we have to get the hang of the fact that this is a quiz show and that there will be amusing banter between the contestant, Jamal, and the host, Prem, who as it turns out, is a classic "frenemy." Next, we realize that the stakes grow higher with each of the ten questions, both quantitatively, as the amount of money to be gained or lost increases, and emotionally, as we become more invested in our beleaguered protagonist.

Because we have such a firm grasp on the routine—what we might call the structure—through the use of repetition, we can introduce important and pleasurable variations. The flashbacks in *Slumdog Millionaire* grow longer, as you can see in the series grid on p. 45: i.e. more time elapses between iterations #5 and #7. Here, the structure is so solid it can allow for this kind of expansion in depth and detail.

There are other variations in the *Q & A* series: sometimes the answer precedes the question; or there isn't a flashback at all, but, instead, Jamal uses one of his three lifelines: "Ask the Audience" (where he can tell from the crowd's cheering which answer he should pick), "50/50" (where two of the four answers disappear, greatly increasing his chances of guessing correctly), and "Phone a Friend" (where he can make one telephone call to solicit advice).

A central series can take advantage of such structural variations to create relatively superficial interest, but a strong central series can also introduce important variations in content. In fact, the tighter the core of the repetitions, the more amazing and intense can be the variations.

For example, the 16,000-rupee question is: "In depictions of the god Rama, he is famously holding what in his right hand? Is it A) a flower, B) a scimitar, C) a child, or D) a bow and arrow?"

This is the third iteration of the *Q & A* series, and it is by far the most serious; Jamal knows the answer because he and his brother, Salim, watched their mother get murdered in a riot on the Hindu holiday that celebrates the birth of Rama. This violence and heartbreak, which deals with such a large topic as religious enmity in a highly factionalized country (the boys belong to the Muslim minority in Mumbai), are represented by one of the most surreal images in the film (a picture of a Hindu boy about their age completely covered in blue body paint and holding a bow and arrow). Because this scene is strongly networked to the *Q & A* series, it is taken in stride by the audience as a high point and not any kind of an outlier.

For this reason, thinking about a present timeline that answers the most basic question as the central series is more valuable than thinking of it as the plot. Though it performs a basic function to tell the story, it is really the meeting point of all the other series that are woven in to it, such as how the inhabitants of the slums in India are treated and still survive, whether true love can triumph, and what is the nature of family loyalty. That's a lot of variety, emerging from the very scenes that are the fabric of this film. That's why it's just easier to call everything a series.

The Central Series Has to Reflect the Theme

So far, we have seen that the central series is the easiest to track, asks the most basic question, and returns us to the present timeline. The central series also has to reflect the theme, as do all of your series.

Let us recall the mantra: Your book can only be about one thing, and we call that your theme. It's then up to your series to develop and convey the depth, complexity, and richness of your theme.

The theme of *Slumdog Millionaire* is stated on the night Jamal is arrested on suspicion of fraud. After making no progress trying to get Jamal to confess, the exasperated police inspector finally blurts out:

> INSPECTOR
> Professors, lawyers, doctors,
> General Knowledge Wallahs* never
> get beyond sixteen thousand
> rupees. And he's on *ten million*?
> What the hell can a slumdog
> possibly know?

---

* Guys, or blokes.

What the hell can a slumdog possibly know? The central series supports this theme with obviously identifiable symbols such as Alexandre Dumas's novel *The Three Musketeers* or the location of Cambridge Circus in British urban geography. But the theme is present not only in the content (what Jamal knows) but also in the form, as we see what happens when Jamal does not know something.

In the ninth and second-to-last iteration of the *Q & A* series, Jamal is being honest when he says that he does not know the answer to the 10-million-rupee question:

> PREM
> Which cricketer has scored the most first-class centuries in history? Was it A) Sachin Tendulkar, B) Ricky Ponting, C) Michael Slater, or D) Jack Hobbs.

Prem is the game show host who has risen from the untouchable caste to a life of riches through celebrity. Viewers are unsure whether or not Prem supports Jamal's efforts on the quiz show. Does Prem want to be the only "slumdog millionaire"? This is the question asked by the *Prem* series: Is he on Jamal's side, or not? The iterations of the *Prem* series lead us in both directions. At one point Prem seems to give Jamal actual advice, if not encouragement, with his speech about what someone from the lowest caste in rigid Indian society needs to make it to the top. (One criterion: "steel balls.") He seems to support Jamal in a scene that takes place in the lavatory after the 10-million-rupee question has been asked (but not yet answered):

> PREM
> A guy from the slums becomes a millionaire overnight. You know the only other person who's done

that? Me. I know what it's like.
I know what you've been through.

JAMAL
I'm not going to become a
millionaire. I don't know the
answer.

PREM
You've said that before, yaar.

JAMAL
No, I really don't.

PREM
What? You can't take the money
and run now. You're on the edge
of history, kid!

JAMAL
I don't see what else I can do.

PREM
Maybe it is written, my friend.
You're going to win this.
Trust me, you're going to win.

After this scene, the stage direction reads as follows: "Prem leaves.
Jamal flushes and comes out of the cubicle. Goes to the washbasins.
In the mist on the mirror above the taps is written the letter 'B.' Jamal
stares at it. Gradually it fades, leaving only the growing fury on his
face staring back at him."

Fury, why, what? My fifteen-year-old daughter is smarter than I am because she smelled a rat right away, whereas I hadn't during my first viewing. Jamal returns to the set and uses his "50/50" lifeline to take away two answers, leaving him to guess between B and D.

This is when it is worthwhile to recall the theme of the film as posed by the Inspector: "What the hell can a slumdog possibly know?" The central series has to reflect the theme just as every other series does. Jamal doesn't know the answer to the question but he knows not to trust the game show host, and, eventually, we in the audience catch on. Because 'B' was written in the fog on the bathroom mirror, Jamal knows the answer now is 'D.' He knows from experience that things are not always as they seem, the very definition of street smarts, perhaps.

It is not so much *what* a slumdog knows as *how* a slumdog comes to know that is what the film has been about.

Getting Hands-on:

Find your central series, one that uses the three criteria presented above: it is easy to track, it asks a basic question, and it establishes the present timeline of your work. You can use time stamps, such as months or seasons passing, but it is better to find a series that enters the action at some point and reflects the theme.

One question you will want to consider with every series is whether you put the iterations in chronological order (the order in which they happened) or in narrative order (a different order for the sake of presentation). Note now how you will handle each of your series, and remember, if you are working with multiple timelines, your reader stands a better chance of figuring out the overall narrative order if each individual series is presented in chronological order.

Chapter Four

Using Series to Reveal the Theme in *The Social Network,* screenplay by Aaron Sorkin

With this chapter, we have reached the halfway point of the book. We have seen several examples of the series grid, that tool that will eventually replace the traditional outline as it gets wider and longer. We have seen a few examples of the series arc, that tool that will give you a proactive way to plot your book's structure, without privileging events above types of series such as character, relationship, location, symbol, and philosophy. In this chapter, the third (and final) tool of Book Architecture will be introduced: the series target. The series grid will tell you how well spaced the iterations of your series are, and the series arc will give you the emotional reality of following a series. The series target—with your theme at the bull's-eye—that will tell you whether a series belongs at all. But first a little bit longer of a warm-up is needed.

In Chapter One, we talked about how many iterations of a series are necessary and how many might be valuable. In Chapter Two, we explored how a series is the most powerful way to display character. In Chapter Three, we discussed using series to deploy multiple timelines. We'll go through all of these concepts again here using Aaron Sorkin's 2010 screenplay for the film *The Social Network* as our example both to solidify and augment our understanding of series and as a way to provide an adequate synopsis of Sorkin's film.

A Series Works Through Multiple Iterations

When we talk about the number of iterations that a series should have, we know that it must have at least two. *The Social Network* demonstrates a very powerful example of a two-iteration series, bookending practically the entire film. We'll call that series *Is Mark an Asshole?* Mark is Mark Zuckerberg, the genius but socially inept Harvard student behind the founding of the now mega-social media site Facebook. His girlfriend at the beginning of the film is Erica Albright, a student who attends Boston University (BU).

In the first scene, they break up, and Erica offers him this clarification:

> ERICA
> You are probably going to be a very successful computer person. But you're going to go through life thinking that girls don't like you because you're a nerd. And I want you to know, from the bottom of my heart, that that won't be true. It'll be because you're an asshole.   (p. 10)

In the very last scene—nearly two hours later in the film—we get the second and only other iteration of this series. The scene involves Marylin, the second-year junior associate who advises Mark to settle out of court on both of the lawsuits that resulted from the explosive success of Facebook. She tells him:

MARYLIN
You're not an asshole, Mark.
You're just trying so hard to be.   (p. 163)

More than 150 pages in the screenplay later (or 110 minutes of running time in a 120-minute movie) and the second iteration registers just as clearly as if the first one had been just a few pages before. There is no formula that I know of that teaches you to bookend two powerful iterations of a series this way, but it works for this film.

Any variety of numbers of iterations can work, from two to as many as your reader/viewer can remember. I made the point earlier in the "Corduroy" chapter, that only when you have three iterations can you actually plot a narrative arc. Between two iterations you can only have a straight line.

Let's look at the narrative arc of a three-iteration series, *Erica & Mark*. We have already seen the first iteration above, where Erica clarifies why girls won't like Mark and then leaves the bar (p. 10). The second iteration comes exactly in the middle of the film (p. 77–80 of a 164-page screenplay). Mark runs into Erica at a club but can't convince her to leave the table where she is dining with her friends so that he can properly apologize to her. The third iteration of this series comes at the very end of the film (p. 162–63) as Mark continues to refresh his computer screen to see if Erica Albright has accepted his friend request on Facebook.

The irony of this last scene is magical. Mark has become the youngest billionaire in the world on account of Facebook's success. Yet the site that eventually got him into the exclusive upper society he wanted so badly to be a part of is also what has allowed Erica to exclude him from her life by not friending him. It is certainly not a happy ending. We'll talk more about the theme of exclusivity in a bit, but what makes this last scene possible is the *Erica & Mark* series, a perfectly spaced three-iteration series that puts the *architecture* part in Book Architecture as far as I'm concerned. Let's graph the series arc of the *Erica & Mark* series to appreciate its sweep.

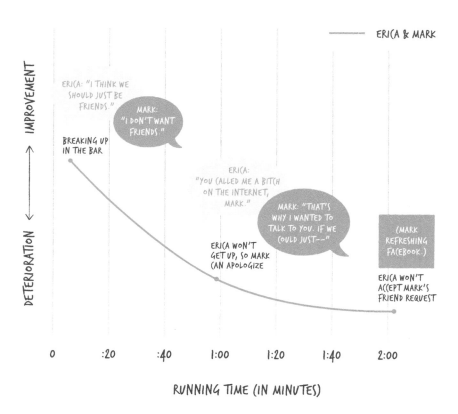

founder of Napster who slides his way into owning a sizable share of Facebook, discuss how many iterations of a particular series there should be (the *I'm CEO . . . Bitch* series).

> Sorkin: If we only hear it once, which we do earlier,
>   is that enough payoff for the end?
> Timberlake: [When] it only came up once, I was
>   making a bigger to-do about it.
> Sorkin: So you think we can land it only doing it
>   once (before)?
> Timberlake: I . . . I think so.
> Sorkin: Great.

That is exactly the kind of question we must ask ourselves when we do series work. How much can a reader or a viewer remember? How obvious do we want something to be, especially because people don't like when something is *too* obvious? If you are using multiple timelines, the memory of the audience may be further compromised, advocating for an extra reminder here or there. Like *Slumdog Millionaire*, *The Social Network* uses three different timelines, which we will look at after we recap how series help build some of the important characters in the film.

Series Is the Best Way to Reveal Character

In the context of *The Great Gatsby,* we discussed how series bring out the best (and worst) in your characters. In a film, you have even less time to establish a character in a viewer's mind, to use series to demonstrate a change in state, rather than just focusing on symbolic behavior in a particular scene. Each of the major characters from *The Social Network* below has a particular series that introduces them, develops their character, and contains some resolution. I have written out several series sentences for each to give some added context by way of a synopsis; ideally, each series would be described in one sentence indicating the change that they undergo or the tension that they represent.

- Cameron Winklevoss: One of two twins who row crew for Harvard—the "Winklevei," as Mark refers to them together. These brothers live in the upper echelons of society and epitomize everything Mark wants; Mark allegedly steals their idea for a website, resulting in the founding of Facebook. But Cameron doesn't want to sue Mark until all other avenues have been exhausted, believing that is not what *Gentlemen of Harvard* do. The *Gentlemen of Harvard* series ends 80 percent of the way through the film when Cameron changes his mind: "Screw it. Let's gut the freakin' nerd."

- Eduardo Saverin: Eduardo is Mark's best friend and cofounder/CFO of Facebook. He gives Mark the start-up money and later sues Mark for forcing him out of the majority of his Facebook shares. Eduardo's character is defined by the *Eduardo's Father* series. It takes a lot to make Eduardo's father proud, apparently, and this series becomes our defining perspective on this character. "You have no idea what that's going to mean to my father." "I'm going to have to explain this to my father." "My father won't even look at me." Extrapolating from this, we surmise that pleasing his father is why Eduardo takes an internship in New York instead of traveling to Palo Alto with Mark, why he wants to monetize the site early and often . . . pretty much why he does everything.

- Christy: Christy is Eduardo's girlfriend. "Christy's crazy," Eduardo tells Mark. That's actually the third iteration of the series that begins with her wearing a very low-cut blouse to the Bill Gates speech and then having sex with Eduardo in a public restroom. The fourth and last iteration is when she sets her new scarf on fire in a garbage can on Eduardo's bed, proving that, yes, *Christy's Crazy.*

- Sean Parker: Some of the iterations of the *Sean as a Wild Card* series feel planted to me, I have to confess. Or maybe that's just my Sean Parker paranoia speaking! Eduardo's the first one on to Sean: "He's had a reputation with drugs . . ." Eduardo reminds Mark that "[t]he drugs, the girls" were enough to get Sean crashed out of two Internet companies already. Then we see the after-party at Kappa Eta Sigma, which results in a drug bust. The set directions read: "One of the policemen casually takes Sean's hand and sees that his palm looks like he just used it to erase a blackboard. Sean says: 'That's not mine.'"

You will notice that I left Mark out of the discussion above. That is because, as we first saw in the *Gatsby* chapter, a main character, also called a round character, will always have more than one series. Everybody needs a series; we can't just hear about what they're like. With a main/round character like Mark, we need more than one. We need to see him idolize *Those Who Row Crew*, be obsessed with *Getting Into Final Clubs* (the undergraduate social clubs at Harvard), and constantly *Subvert Authority*, whether it be Harvard's Administrative Board, potential investors, or opposing legal counsel.

Series Help You Use Multiple Timelines

In Chapter Three, we looked at *Slumdog Millionaire* and saw how, when a narrative uses three timelines, readers/viewers choose one timeline and equate that to the present. We called this the central series. *The Social Network* also uses three timelines, so it needs a strong central series that will be easy to track, return us to the present timeline, and serve the theme. In this case, the central series is the founding and evolution of Facebook as shown through its exponential growth in terms of the number of its members, the number of schools where it is popular, and, eventually, the number of countries where it is available.

THE SOCIAL NETWORK:
SERIES GRID

ITERATION NUMBER	PAGE NUMBER	SERIES NAME: FACEBOOK MEMBERS SERIES TYPE: CENTRAL	
1	55	1 (MARK)	
2	59	"AS OF YESTERDAY EVENING, ZUCKERBERG SAID OVER 650 STUDENTS HAD REGISTERED TO USE THEFACEBOOK.COM. HE SAID HE ANTICIPATED THAT 900 STUDENTS WOULD HAVE JOINED THE SITE BY THIS MORNING."	
3	71	4,000 MEMBERS	
4	80	EXPANDING TO YALE AND COLUMBIA. "AND STANFORD."	
5	102	29 SCHOOLS AND 75,000 MEMBERS	
6	112	BREAKING THE 150,000-MEMBER BARRIER.	
7	123	SEAN: "A HUNDRED SCHOOLS BY THE END OF THE SUMMER?... TELL YOU WHAT, GESTURE OF GOOD FAITH. WHILE YOU'RE GETTING INTO A HUNDRED SCHOOLS, I'LL PUT YOU ON TWO CONTINENTS."	
8	135	160 SCHOOLS AND 300,000 MEMBERS	
9	152	A MILLION MEMBERS, AND EVERYTHING THAT HAPPENS AROUND THAT.	
10	163	POSTSCRIPT SUPERIMPOSED ON THE SCREEN: "FACEBOOK HAS 500 MILLION MEMBERS IN 207 COUNTRIES. IT'S CURRENTLY VALUED AT 25 BILLION DOLLARS. MARK ZUCKERBERG IS THE YOUNGEST BILLIONAIRE IN THE WORLD."	

As a central series, the *Facebook Members* series does a good job of helping us keep track of our progress through the film. It communicates the emotional tone of the moment, and it lets us build to the "Millionth Member Party" as the climax of the film. It also lets us know what's at stake; as one of the taglines for the film reads, "You can't get to 500 million friends without making a few enemies."

There is great variation in the *Facebook Members* central series, which is always crucial so things don't appear so cookie-cutter. We've already discussed number of members, colleges, and countries, but how about also adding in the number of continents, who's delivering the news about the most recent growth spurt, whether that news is delivered by a character or is visually represented, whether it is aspirational or actual, and whether or not it means anything at all in the big scheme of life.

The story of the founding and evolution of Facebook is that of an exponential rise in terms of its popularity and the wealth of the company. The *Facebook Members* series lets us track that. In the same way, each of the other two timelines contain something that is easy for us to track, so that, when we jump off and on these timelines, we know where we are when we get back.

In other words, each timeline has its own version of a central series. In the *Winklevoss Lawsuit* timeline, it is the number of emails and phone messages by which Cameron, Tyler, and their colleague, Divya, try to get in touch with Mark; as the number of correspondences unreturned by Mark mounts, so does the evidence that Mark has indeed defrauded them of some form of intellectual property. In the *Eduardo Lawsuit* timeline, we keep track of the four "punches" (a form of hazing) that are required for Eduardo's admission into the Phoenix Club. Each of these other two timelines operate the same way the *Facebook Members* series does by giving us something concrete by which to keep time. Anything that can help us feel reasonably secure that we will remember where we are can help you take us beyond the boundaries of what we can see.

Because the central series of *The Social Network,* the number of *Facebook Members,* is so strong, it not only allows us to recognize the present timeline, but it also allows for flashbacks and flash-forwards as this story is told in narrative order instead of chronological order.

If *The Social Network* had been presented in chronological order, it would have begun in the fall of 2003, and that timeline would be the only one we'd see until the two lawsuits were engaged. After that, the two lawsuits would take over until the very end, when all three timelines would exist simultaneously. That kind of chronological order might be visually represented like this:

THE SOCIAL NETWORK: MULTIPLE TIMELINES

However, if we arrange these three timelines in terms of how they appear in the film's narrative order, we get a much more dynamic interplay between elements. In the following diagram, each scene is color-coded to one of the three timelines. You can see the variation in terms of which timeline we get to visit; you can also see that each timeline itself proceeds straight through in chronological order.

THE SOCIAL NETWORK:
NARRATIVE ORDER OF SCENIC PRESENTATION

1	2	1	3	1	4	5	6	2	2	3	3	4	4	7	5	8	6	9
7	10	5	6	11	7	12	8	13	9	14	10	15	11	16	17	18	19	20
12	8	13	21	22	23	14	24	25	26	9	27	28	29	10	30	11	31	12
32	13	33	14	34	15	35	16	36	17	37	18	38	39	19	40	41	42	43
44	45	46	47	20	48	49	21	50	22	51	52	53	54	23	15	24	55	

▓ FOUNDING OF FACEBOOK
▓ EDUARDO LAWSUIT
▓ WINKLEVOSS LAWSUIT

In the last chapter, I made the recommendation that, if you are working with multiple timelines, and you are presenting your material in narrative order (i.e., events rearranged for dramatic effect), each individual timeline should be presented in chronological order (i.e., the events in the order that they "happened"). *The Social Network* is an example of this recommendation. Though the overall order is a technicolor fabric that challenges the viewer, each event within an individual timeline proceeds directly after another, thereby easing the strain of multiple timelines.

And so there ends our recap of how *The Social Network* embodies the first three chapters before we get to the role of series in revealing theme. Some warm-up, huh?

The Theme of *The Social Network*

How do we go about finding the theme of *The Social Network*? If this were a class, we would first list all of the series sentences from *The Social Network*. Then we would arrange them in a top-down order of importance; this ordering is done by instinct and can sometimes be influenced by the number of iterations that comprise a series (more equals more important) or the placement of those iterations in important moments such as the beginning or the end. Taking the top four sentences in our order, we would start combining like elements to reduce those four sentences to two sentences, and finally to a single-sentence description of what the film is about, because the film can only be about one thing[*].

Since this is not a class, I'm going to do it for you. Ready? Eduardo says:

> "See, in a world where social structure was everything, that (the ability to invite—or not invite—friends to join Facebook) was *the* thing." (p. 41)

Exclusivity, in other words. Think about it: every series, every scene we have reviewed in the film thus far, eventually points to this one sentence. It seems to be human nature to want to put those one or two sentences into one's narrative that will explain the whole thing. Finding yours can be an "aha" moment.

Draw the Target

Once we have the theme, we can use our third tool, the series target, and place all of our series closer to or farther from the bull's-eye based on their individual relevance to theme. Initially, this is done by instinct when you're in an early draft, but, eventually, this kind of visual representation can be the very guiding light by which you complete your revision. If you aren't sure if you have come up with the right theme or not, you can draw a few different targets and choose the one that seems to work the best. When we place our series closer to or farther away from the center, we might start with those we think are the

---

[*]   For an extended look at this process, see Chapter Five of *Blueprint Your Bestseller,* "Your One Thing."

most reflective of the theme. If there are arrows that miss the target altogether, the ones just lying in the dust, they might be our "darlings" that need to be "killed" (for a visual representation of this and a longer discussion, see p. 134–136). In the case of *The Social Network*, there are very few, if any, that won't make the target in some fashion.

THE SOCIAL NETWORK: TARGET ONE

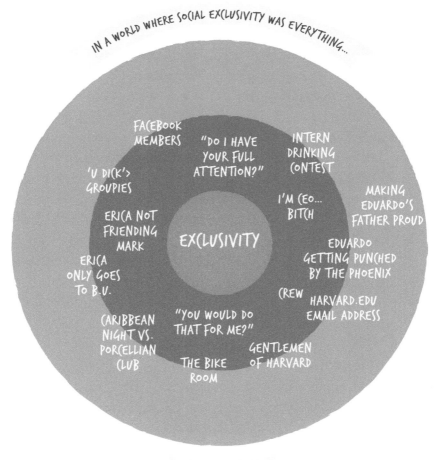

IN A WORLD WHERE SOCIAL EXCLUSIVITY WAS EVERYTHING...

FACEBOOK MEMBERS

"DO I HAVE YOUR FULL ATTENTION?"

INTERN DRINKING CONTEST

'U DICK'> GROUPIES

I'M CEO... BITCH

MAKING EDUARDO'S FATHER PROUD

ERICA NOT FRIENDING MARK

EXCLUSIVITY

ERICA ONLY GOES TO B.U.

EDUARDO GETTING PUNCHED BY THE PHOENIX

CREW   HARVARD.EDU EMAIL ADDRESS

CARIBBEAN NIGHT VS. PORCELLIAN CLUB

"YOU WOULD DO THAT FOR ME?"

GENTLEMEN OF HARVARD

THE BIKE ROOM

...THAT WAS THE THING

In the above diagram, you can see how series will tend to cluster together and suggest others that also might go on the target. Some of these elements we have discussed before, but for any that are new:

- *Harvard.edu* (series type: object): "The most prestigious e-mail address in the country." Because? "Girls wanna get with guys who go to Harvard." This series takes an ironic turn when the Winklevosses' family lawyer can't access their incipient version of the site because he didn't go to Harvard. Cameron says, "That's what we'll do, Mr. Hotchkiss. We'll put all this together and we'll e-mail it to you. . . . You won't be able to get on the website yourself . . . Because you don't have—a Harvard, umm—You know what, it would just be easier for us to e-mail it to you."

- *Porcellian Club versus Caribbean Night* (series type: location): The Porcellian Club is a continuation of harvard.edu. In the words of the club president: "You are at one of the oldest, one of the most exclusive clubs—not just at Harvard but in the world." That exclusivity is not found on Caribbean Night at the Jewish fraternity, depicted visually by all of the empty space between the game hat-wearing partygoers. Nonetheless, it is at this party that Mark entices Eduardo to cofound Facebook with him, starting them both on the upward climb to utter exclusivity.

- *"U dick">groupies* (series type: relationship): As the Porcellian Club seems to indicate, when you get on the right side/the inside of exclusivity, you get the girls. This series shows Mark and Eduardo's popularity and dating fortunes. First, Mark does "this thing" where he manages to get all girls to hate them, symbolized by the anonymous note passed to Mark in operating systems class that reads simply: "U dick." Eventually, though, Eduardo giddily tells Mark: "We have groupies."

This takes care of most of the series on the target above, and if we haven't hit them all, well, we have to leave *something* for the students who have done all their homework. Besides, I want to make a different point right now, which is that, even when we turn to some of the minor characters or scenes which seem to be in the film for another purpose, everything breathes *exclusivity*. This movie is tight.

THE SOCIAL NETWORK:
TARGET TWO

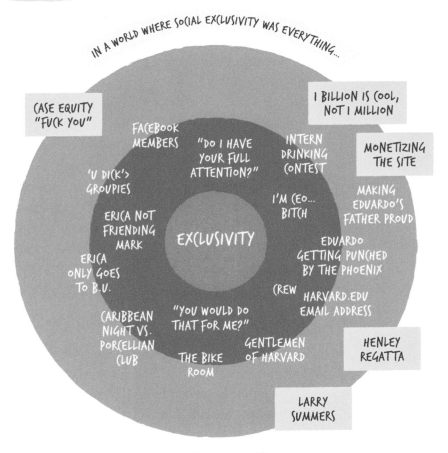

IN A WORLD WHERE SOCIAL EXCLUSIVITY WAS EVERYTHING...

CASE EQUITY
"FUCK YOU"

FACEBOOK MEMBERS

"DO I HAVE YOUR FULL ATTENTION?"

INTERN DRINKING CONTEST

I BILLION IS COOL, NOT I MILLION

MONETIZING THE SITE

'U DICK'> GROUPIES

ERICA NOT FRIENDING MARK

I'M CEO... BITCH

MAKING EDUARDO'S FATHER PROUD

EXCLUSIVITY

EDUARDO GETTING PUNCHED BY THE PHOENIX

ERICA ONLY GOES TO B.U.

CREW HARVARD.EDU EMAIL ADDRESS

CARIBBEAN NIGHT VS. PORCELLIAN CLUB

"YOU WOULD DO THAT FOR ME?"

GENTLEMEN OF HARVARD

HENLEY REGATTA

THE BIKE ROOM

LARRY SUMMERS

...THAT WAS THE THING

Let's look at some of these nearly extraneous elements that I have just added.

- *Larry Summers* (series type: character): "Anne?" "Yes sir." "Punch me in the face." That's one of my favorite lines in the movie, uttered by the president of Harvard during a meeting with the Winklevosses, which the twins had requested. But this scene also clearly communicates exclusivity. Summers wants to know how they got this meeting (how they got this far inside a different rung of exclusivity where they don't belong). Additionally, Summers' administrative assistant describes the building that houses Summers' office as "a hundred years older than the country it's in. So do be careful."

- *Henley Royal Regatta Reception Room* (series type: location): A key scene in England during one of the most prestigious rowing events in the world. It not only reveals that Facebook has spread "across the pond" but also symbolically depicts the necessity of getting there first—whether you are competitive rowers or developing a website, nobody remembers who came in second. It also radiates exclusivity, from the posh blazers worn by the Winklevoss boys to the fact that Prince Albert—whose social status outranks everybody in the room—cuts them off and moves on after chatting for less than a minute.

- *Case Equity "Fuck You"* (series type: phrase): The venture capitalists at Case Equity want to invest in Facebook, but Mark turns them down at the behest of Sean Parker; Case Equity has made the mistake of turning their back on Sean before, and now they must pay. Sean preps Mark: "They're gonna pitch you . . . They're gonna beg you to take their money." Mark does as instructed and shows up in his bathrobe and slippers, asking members of Case Equity: "Which one of you is Mitchell Manningham?" He follows this with "Sean Parker says 'Fuck you.'" Mark and Sean are now the exclusive ones.

- *$1B is Cool, Not $1M* (series type: phrase): Sean advises Eduardo not to monetize the site yet, because not only would it mean taking the coolest party in town and ending it at eleven but also because "[a] million dollars isn't cool. You know what's cool . . . A billion dollars."

We could go on. As we noted at the beginning of the chapter, Mark's creation of Facebook, the thing that eventually gets him into that exclusive upper society he so badly wants to be a part of, is also what eventually allows Erica to exclude him (by not friending him). Facebook is also the thing that cuts Mark off from his only true friend, Eduardo. The beast he created has turned against him, so to speak. Exclusivity has its price.

I'm going to go ahead and say that every minute of *The Social Network* contains the theme of exclusivity in one form or another. From Eduardo getting punched by the Phoenix, which Mark agrees might just be a diversity thing (i.e., that's the only way Eduardo's getting that far inside something so exclusive), to Mark's explanation of why the Winklevosses are suing him: "[They] aren't suing me for intellectual property theft. They're suing me because, for the first time in their lives, things didn't work out the way they were supposed to for them."

Sometimes you want to be subtle with your theme, such as when Mark is interviewed by the *Crimson*, the Harvard student newspaper, that reports, "Zuckerberg said that he hoped the privacy options would help to restore his reputation following student outrage over Facemash.com [the website Mark creates in the opening minutes of the film that compares the relative hotness of two girls at a time]." Tyler Winklevoss sees this quote of Mark's as a direct challenge, an indicator of *who's exclusive now*: "That's exactly what *we* said to him. He's giving us the finger in the *Crimson*!"

Other times you just want to call your theme right out there. Eduardo sees that Mark's idea for Facebook "would be exclusive." Mark says, "You'd have to know the people on the site to get past your own page. Like getting punched."

Now I know what you may be thinking: Does every series have to fit on the archery target? This is like asking, "Does every series have to belong to the theme?" What about tangential series, those that are not so "on the nose"? What about the whimsical, the just-because? The digressions that are "the soul of reading," as Laurence Sterne once said?

Well, you do what you want. I'm just saying that readers/viewers want series that are well networked to the theme (pun not intentional, but it works) so that they can make sense of the narrative with which they are presented. Once we have the theme, we can then examine every series for its aptness, for its fullness, and for its relationship to other series. Working with series that reflect the theme also makes it much easier to create an extended series grid, as we will encounter in the next chapter.

Getting Hands-on:

Arrange your series sentences in a top-down order of importance; then take the top four sentences and combine their elements to reduce the theme to two sentences and finally to a single-sentence description of what your manuscript is about—your theme.

Place your theme in the bull's-eye of a series target (either hand-drawn or using a software program such as Scapple), and place all of your series closer to or farther from the theme, based on their relevance. If you are having trouble getting a series onto the target at all, you might be looking at an aspect of your narrative that you can just as well do without.

Chapter Five

The Expanded Series Grid in J. K. Rowling's *Harry Potter and the Order of the Phoenix*

Now that you have developed a fairly good grasp on identifying your series, as well as checked them for their relevancy against your theme through the tool of the series target, you are ready for an advanced look at the series grid. An expanded series grid allows you to plan the gaps between iterations in a given series, thereby creating the effects of foreshadowing and suspense; it allows you to visualize how your series interact and intersect so that you can weave disparate series into a unified whole; and it enables you to find the key scenes where the most series are present, which is what prompts the emotional pay-off for the reader—that feeling it is "all coming together."

For this chapter on the series grid, I'd like to invite in C. S. Plocher as a coauthor. C.S. is a noted Potter scholar at the website writelikerowling.com and has read the entire Harry Potter series "comfortably" close to ten times. (Here, I use the word "series" in its more conventional meaning, to which we will return soon.) I first fell in love with C.S. when she did a four-part blog series on J. K. Rowling and the Book Architecture Method; my favorite line: "Rowling obviously agrees with Horwitz because look at how she structured her outline for *The Order of the Phoenix* . . ." Everything after this introductory paragraph comes from the both of us, hence our use of "we." "I" is still me, and "C.S.," well, is C.S.

J. K. Rowling's Series Grid

I know we said that every narrative discussed would be adequately synopsized, but that's difficult with this 870-page beast of a book. Here's our best shot at it: Fifteen-year-old Harry is trying to cram for the wizard equivalent of the SATs, but distractions keep popping up, such as attempting to navigate his first romantic relationship with the pretty Cho Chang, helping his soft-hearted friend Hagrid tame his wild half-brother, leading an illegal defense group against the intolerable High Inquisitor Dolores Umbridge, and, of course, fighting a life-or-death battle against the most evil wizard of all time. That's the gist of it anyway.

We are using the fifth book of the seven Harry Potter books simply because that is the only volume for which Rowling revealed a glimpse of her outlining techniques—and because said outline "proves" the importance of understanding and using series to write a book.

Here's the original handwritten outline:

Don't worry if you can't read it because there's a transcribed version of this outline later in the chapter. For now, let's just regard this wondrous artifact and lay out its basic components. In the first column, we have numbers ranging from 13 to 24; these were the original chapter numbers before Rowling switched things up. As I have said, you can use scene numbers here if you have broken your work down to that level of granularity, or you can use your chapters as Rowling did in creating her series grid. Whatever designation permits an effective division within your narrative can be used to help you examine a particular set of pages against the whole and thereby be able to do some good in the creation and revision process.

Next to the chapter numbers we have a progression of months from October through April, what I called a "time stamp" in Chapter Three. Next to those two columns, we have the chapter title . . . and after that? What are the next seven columns?

Well, they are series, and this is a series grid. Not that Rowling calls it that; she doesn't have to. Remember, *Rowling agrees with Horwitz.* . . .

The Outliners and the Pantsers

You may have heard there is this debate between the outliners, those who plan their work meticulously, and the pantsers, those who write simply by the seat of their pants. Suffice it to say, this is not a real debate. We are all both outliners, even if that outline exists only in our minds, *and* pantsers, because we are constantly discovering something new. The only questions are what proportion we are of each and at what time. This book recommends confiding your outline to paper (or digitally in a spreadsheet) in the form of a series grid at some point. Why put yourself through the struggle of remembering where you are right now when the point is to discover the next horizon of creativity?

It isn't as if a series grid is going to solve all of your writing problems. It just gives you something to work with. One of my favorite writing mantras is "don't start with too much," but another one is "don't start with nothing." In the third iteration of the *Rowling Agrees with Horwitz* series, we can hear Rowling's thoughts on the matter in an interview she did with school children: "I always have a basic plot outline, but I like to leave some things to be decided while I write. It's more fun."* She has also explained why she spent five years prepping for her books before attempting to write Book One: "I loathe books that have inconsistencies and leave questions unanswered. Loopholes bug the hell out of me."† Continuing in

---

* J.K. Rowling, interview by *Scholastic*, February 3, 2000.
† Jennie Renton, "The Story Behind the Potter Legend," *Sydney Morning Herald*, Oct. 28, 2001.

that thread, she has said: "The five years I spent on *Harry Potter and the Philosopher's Stone* were spent constructing The Rules. I had to lay down all my parameters."[*] Don't start with too much. Don't start with nothing.

One of the ways Rowling does her "constructing" is by creating a series grid. Rowling has said many times that she filled notebook after notebook with plans for her Potter books, so we think it is safe to assume that the grid we are studying here is an excerpt from a larger series grid. When Rowling posted this excerpted grid as an "Easter egg" on her website (something her devoted readers would have to search for), she titled it "Revision of the Plan of *Order of the Phoenix*," and for a description she wrote, "Part of the umpteenth revision of the plan of 'Order of the Phoenix.' Some of the chapter names changed and there are a few ideas that didn't make the final draft." Some of the changes Rowling is referring to were minor, such as turning Grawp into Hagrid's half-brother instead of cousin and switching around the names for Dumbledore's Army and the Order of the Phoenix. But other changes were major, such as delaying Hagrid's return until Umbridge has her regime in full swing and delaying Harry's lessons with Snape until after Mr. Weasley is attacked.

That is the purpose of a series grid: It is a tool. No one is going to grade you on it. It exists *so that* you can change things. What kind of a tool allows you to evolve your work and thereby renders itself obsolete at the same time? It is like creating a map to an unknown territory that you're just discovering. You can continue to update your map, or you can let go of it once you have reached the shore.

---

[*]   J.K., Rowling, "World Exclusive Interview with J K Rowling," *South West News Service,* July 8, 2000.

Harry Potter Series: Rowling's Outline

No.	Time	Title	Plot	Prophecy	Cho / Ginny
13	Oct	Plots and Resistance	Harry has a lesson scheduled with Snape, but he skips it to go to Hogsmeade with Ron and Hermione. They meet Lupin and Tonks but can't talk because Umbridge is tailing them, so they pass a note. Harry, Ron, and Hermione are recruiting for Dumbledore's Army. Hagrid has fresh injuries.	Harry sees the Hall of Prophecy (in a dream). Voldemort is still formulating his plans; none of his Death Eaters are able to get in, so he sends his snake Nagini on a recon mission.	Cho is in Hogsmeade and wants to join Dumbledore's Army.
14	Nov	Dumbledore's Army	First meeting of Dumbledore's Army		Cho and Ginny are both present.
15	Nov	The Dirtiest Tackle	Harry is suspended from Quidditch after he attacks Malfoy because Malfoy taunted him about Cedric. That night Harry is restless and unable to sleep; he worries about Umbridge, Cho, and his scar. Harry sees Nagini attack Mr. Weasley (in a dream).	Nagini attacks Mr. Weasley.	Cho is now madly in love.
16	Nov	Black Marks	Harry rows about skipping his lessons with Snape; Harry is in the doghouse and he's angry. An overview of Christmas. Hermione contacts Rita. Another lesson with Snape.	Nagini gets into the Hall of Prophecy. Voldemort has confirmation of Bode's story – that only he and Harry can touch the prophecy.	Cho kiss? Ginny is concerned about her father.
17	Dec	Rita Returns	Harry, Ron and Hermione go to Hogsmeade for their Christmas shopping and meet with Rita.	Rita supplies information.	Harry is now avoiding Cho a bit. Ginny is with someone else?
18	Dec	St. Mungo's Hospital for Magical Maladies and Injuries	They visit Mr. Weasley at St. Mungo's on Xmas Eve. They also see Macnair visiting Bode and run into Professor Lockhart and Neville.	Now Voldemort is actively trying to get Harry to the Hall of Prophecy. Harry's dreams are very vivid; he can see his name.	Ginny is visiting her dad.
19	Dec	Xmas		Bode's dead.	Hermione's with Krum and Ginny has a boyfriend.
20	Dec	Extended Powers of Elvira Umbridge	Harry misses the Quidditch match against Hufflepuff. Why weren't they at the match? Umbridge now suspects the existence of Dumbledore's Army. Another lesson with Snape?	Harry is fighting increasingly strong visions but not very successfully.	
21	Feb	Valentine's Day	Harry is in Hogsmeade with Cho. Professor Trelawney is fired and Firenze replaces her in the nick of time. Rita reports back on Bode, etc. Another lesson with Snape?	"	Harry has a Valentine's date with Cho; they're miserable and row.
22	Feb	Cousin Grawp	Umbridge is now going after Professor Hagrid. Harry, Ron, and Hermione go to warn Hagrid about Umbridge and they meet Grawp. Firenze is teaching about prophets and prophecies. Another lesson with Snape?	"	
23	Mar	Treason	At Easter Dumbledore's Army is discovered; Dumbledore takes the rap for it – Azkaban.		Cho wants back with Harry, but they row again.
24	Apr	Careers Guidance	At his career consultation Harry is interested in being an Auror. Dumbledore's Army continues meeting. Ginny is angry. Harry has a lesson with Snape.	Harry starting to get how to block his dreams.	

Order of the Phoenix	Dumbledore's Army	Snape / Harry + Father	Hagrid + Grawp
Tonks and Lupin	Recruiting	Harry skips his lesson to recruit for Dumbledore's Army.	Hagrid's still being injured and has blood stains. ("He's feeding something that's not his blood.")
Umbridge is now reading their mail.	First meeting	Harry's still skipping his lessons.	"
"			"
Firehead			
Ron and the rest of the Weasleys are told about their father's injury.	Reactions to the attack — another meeting and an overview?	A row about Harry not going to his lessons	Hagrid's still getting injured.
		Another lesson	Hagrid's in the hospital wing.
They're around.			
Sirius is here; there's a big reunion.			
Sirius and Lupin	Big meeting	In his lesson with Snape, Harry mentions the Hall of Prophecy.	Hagrid's out of the hospital and going into the Forbidden Forest armed with spikes, etc.
"			
Gone here		Snape gets angry at Harry because Harry can't do it.	
"			
Firehead	See plot. Meeting.	Snape grudgingly approves.	Hagrid's clinging to his job and refusing to abandon Grawp.

Rowling's Series Grid Transcribed

You will remember when I asked you in Chapter One to remove the word outline from your writer's vocabulary. I did so because the word "outline" brings to mind one fatal flaw: it implies something linear, while a series grid is spatial. When people think of an outline, they think of the legal enumerations that they learned in school. Here's that kind of outline for this chapter so far:

1. Introduction
   a. Ready for an expanded grid
   b. Introducing C. S. Plocher
2. Using Potter Volume Five
   a. No real synopsis offered
   b. The reason we are using Book Five is because of her outline
3. Rowling's outline
   a. The first two columns show chapter numbers and a time stamp
   b. The rest of the columns are her series
4. Outliners vs. Pantsers
   a. "Don't Start with Too Much/Nothing"
   b. Rowling changed some things since this series grid
5. The series grid is spatial in nature

I don't know about you, but I don't find that kind of outline inviting. It doesn't entice me to consider how all of the elements I am writing about are part of the same thing. Because, in the end, that's what we're after: unity. "Organic" may be an overused word nowadays, but anything that has life exists by the whole being bigger than the sum of its parts—and that requires the parts to work together in a way that feels organic: natural, inescapable, inevitable. That is what a series grid can help you accomplish.

When C.S. transcribed Rowling's series grid she cleaned it up a little, adding punctuation and writing out incomplete words, so it would be more readable to Potter outsiders like you (maybe) and me (definitely).

Along the horizontal x-axis after the chapter number, the time stamp, and the chapter title, there are seven more columns. The first of these seven is disturbingly labeled Plot. We'll get to this in a very short while and explain why it isn't really the traditional "plot" that Rowling is referring to. The last six columns are the series that Rowling is tracking in her grid. Here is a short description of each of these six series:

- *Hall of Prophecy:* The location where the Order of the Phoenix (the good guys) are protecting a mysterious but important weapon that Voldemort (the evil guy) is trying to steal. Because of Harry's as-of-yet unexplained connection to Voldemort's thoughts, Harry has many strange dreams about the Hall of Prophecy and the weapon hidden inside it.

- *Cho/Ginny:* Cho is Harry's first ever attempt at a romantic relationship—and it's a disaster. Rowling subtly juxtaposes this relationship to Harry's much more natural budding romance with Ginny, which doesn't fully surface until Book Six.

- *Dumbledore's Army:* A secret Defense Against the Dark Arts group formed by Harry and his friends in order to 1) resist the new Nazi-esque regime at their school, and 2) prepare themselves to fight the rising power of Voldemort.

- *Order of the Phoenix:* A group of adult witches and wizards formed and led by Dumbledore (the greatest good wizard of all time) whose purpose is to fight and defeat Voldemort.[*]

- *Snape/Harry+Father:* In this series, we finally get a glimpse at the suspicious Professor Snape's past and a partial explanation

---

[*] Remember that in her original series grid, Rowling had the Order of the Phoenix being Harry's secret group and Dumbledore's Army being Dumbledore's group, but she later switched the names. In order to lessen the confusion for those who have read Book Five, we've also swapped the names to match Rowling's final version.

as to why Snape seems to have such an ingrained hatred for Harry, on account of Harry's father.

- *Hagrid+Grawp:* This series follows the soft-hearted Professor Hagrid, who tries to tame seemingly untameable monsters, and whom Harry always somehow gets roped into helping. Hagrid's project this time is his violent half-brother, Grawp.

Series Within a Series

It has no doubt occurred to you that we're talking about series as defined by the Book Architecture Method, while we're also talking about the most popular series of all time, as defined by standard usage, that is, as a collection of books in a particular genre that features many of the same characters. Maybe you have been able to put *that* series out of your mind for most of this book, but, at this point, I think it will be useful to discuss what these two definitions of series actually have in common.

If you are writing a series of books, many series (as defined by Book Architecture) within a single volume will need to be continued throughout the book series as a whole. That's what makes the whole thing cohere. Your series don't all have to take the same form, depending on how abstract they are, but their essence has to repeat. For example, you won't necessarily see an *Order of the Phoenix* series in Books 1–4, but the *Order of the Phoenix* series encompasses a broader series that deals with *Resisting Voldemort*, and that can be found in every book. You also won't find a *Hagrid+Grawp* series in the other Potter books, but there is always a Hagrid series of some sort, whether it involves spiders or dragons or violent half-brothers. This is part of variation on a broader level, and Rowling is particularly adept at it.

Hey, I was never against talking about the *other* series! When considering the necessity of tracking so many series within a given book, I applaud anyone who takes on the process over seven books. That takes some serious planning.

To demonstrate the relationship of a series of books and Book Architecture's series, let's track one of Rowling's series through all seven books. C.S. believes that the easiest and most recognizable series to follow for this purpose is the *Snape* series. This series pretty much stays consistent throughout all seven books, revolving around its main question: Is Snape fighting for the good guys or bad guys?

Below is both an arc and a grid for the *Snape* series. In the *Snape* series arc, you can see how this series exists both before and after Book Five (in light purple), within Book Five but either before or after the snippet of Rowling's series grid we've been studying (in medium purple), and within the series grid of Book Five we are looking at (in dark purple).

HARRY POTTER SERIES:

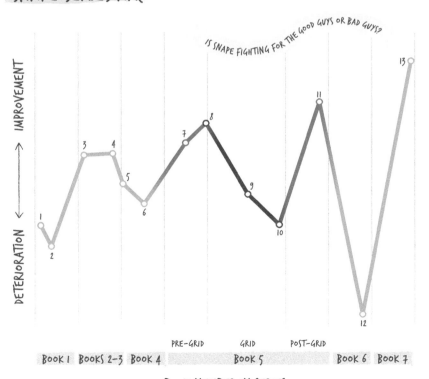

Next, here are the iterations of this series arc described in a little more detail in a series grid.

HARRY POTTER SERIES:
SERIES GRID

ITERATION NUMBER	BOOK NUMBER	SERIES NAME: IS SNAPE FIGHTING FOR THE GOOD GUYS OR BAD GUYS?
1	1	APPEARS THAT SNAPE IS TRYING TO STEAL THE SORCERER'S STONE
2	1	APPEARS THAT SNAPE IS TRYING TO KILL HARRY
3	1	TURNS OUT SNAPE WAS ACTUALLY PROTECTING HARRY AND THE STONE
4	2 & 3	NO DEVELOPMENTS CONCERNING SNAPE'S DUBIOUS LOYALTY
5	4	SNAPE HAVING SECRETIVE CONVERSATIONS WITH A KNOWN DEATH EATER (A FOLLOWER OF VOLDEMORT)
6	4	DISCOVERY THAT SNAPE WAS ONCE A DEATH EATER
7	5, PRE-SERIES GRID	SNAPE IS AN ACTIVE MEMBER OF THE ORDER OF THE PHOENIX
8	5, SERIES GRID	SNAPE GIVES HARRY OCCLUMENCY LESSONS (THE ACT OF MAGICALLY CLOSING ONE'S MIND) TO HELP HARRY DEFEND HIMSELF AGAINST VOLDEMORT
9	5, SERIES GRID	SNAPE REFUSES TO TEACH HARRY ANY MORE OCCLUMENCY
10	5, POST-SERIES GRID	SNAPE APPEARS TO IGNORE HARRY'S PLEA FOR HELP IN PROTECTING HARRY'S GODFATHER
11	5, POST-SERIES GRID	SNAPE ALERTS THE ORDER OF THE PHOENIX TO HARRY'S SITUATION AND EFFECTIVELY SAVES HARRY'S LIFE
12	6	SNAPE KILLS DUMBLEDORE
13	7	REVEALED THAT SNAPE KILLED DUMBLEDORE ON DUMBLEDORE'S ORDERS AND SNAPE DIES PROTECTING HARRY

That is a lot to keep track of and why an expanded series grid is a great idea—especially if you're writing a "series," as in a multivolume set of books—so that you can stay ahead of the game. Rowling posted the handwritten excerpt of her series grid on her website in 2006, three years after Book Five was published. C.S. guesses that Rowling waited this long to release the grid because some of the things mentioned in it don't come to full fruition until later. Rowling didn't want to give anything away, such as Harry's eventual romance with Ginny, which doesn't truly surface until Book Six, but Rowling calls it out in her grid under the series *Cho/Ginny*. Rowling was able to so meticulously plan out seven volumes of storytelling while simultaneously treating each book as an individual entity because she took the time to map out her vision. Tools like the series grid gave her the confidence and flexibility to change major things (such as deciding at the last minute not to have Mr. Weasley die from the snake attack) without worrying it would create a disastrous domino effect for the rest of her story.

That Pesky "Plot" Column

I have to admit, looking at Rowling's series grid, that fourth column labeled "Plot" still upsets me. After all this work, do we still have to talk about plot as if it means something *other* than what we have been talking about the whole time with series? No, we do not. C.S. confirms that Rowling's Plot column is simply where she keeps track of which series are stepping into the spotlight at what time. Imagine that. Rowling's "plot" is her simply taking the individual series in the columns further to the right and figuring out how she'll weave them together in that particular chapter. For example, look at the first row of her grid labeled Chapter 13 and titled "Plots and Resistance."[*]

In the plot column of that row, Rowling writes:

---

[*]   In the published version, this is Chapter 16, "In the Hog's Head."

Harry has a lesson scheduled with Snape, but he skips it to go to Hogsmeade with Ron and Hermione. They meet Lupin and Tonks but can't talk because Umbridge is tailing them, so they pass a note. Harry, Ron, and Hermione are recruiting for Dumbledore's Army. Hagrid has fresh injuries.*

Now take a look at what she writes under each of the individual series to the right of that plot column:

Hall of Prophecy: Harry sees the Hall of Prophecy (in a dream). Voldemort is still formulating his plans; none of his Death Eaters are able to get in, so he sends his snake Nagini on a recon mission.

Cho/Ginny: Cho is in Hogsmeade and wants to join Dumbledore's Army.

Order of the Phoenix: Tonks and Lupin

Dumbledore's Army: Recruiting

Snape/Harry+Father: Harry skips his lesson to recruit for Dumbledore's Army.

Hagrid+Grawp: Hagrid's still being injured and has blood stains.

Now, one more time, let's look at Rowling's Plot column and bold everything that she mentions happening in the "plot" but which is already listed in the individual series columns:

Harry has a lesson scheduled with Snape, but he skips it go to Hogsmeade with Ron and Hermione.

---

* This is from the transcribed version for the sake of readability.

They meet Lupin and Tonks but can't talk because Umbridge is tailing them, so they pass a note. **Harry, Ron, and Hermione are recruiting for Dumbledore's Army. Hagrid has fresh injuries.**

It is almost all bold. What is going on here in this "Plot" column then? Rowling is weaving together her individual series to develop her chapter because, other than a few details she's adding in to flesh out the action (passing a note), she's already written about each of them in the other columns. Rowling is using the "Plot" column to create a simple annotation of what a particular chapter, or scene, will focus on. Therefore, this is not "plot" as something separate from the rest of the narrative but rather just the literal embodiment of my prescription from Chapter Two that a series worth keeping track of needs to enter the action at some point.

When Series Collide

In my first book, when I described what happened when series came together, I used the words "interact" and "intersect." Occasionally I said they would "inform" each other. Pretty tame language in retrospect. In her blog, C.S. does me one better and says that when series come together—especially several of them in a key scene—it is better to say they collide. Series go boom!

Earlier we talked about how the series grid is a tool. You're allowed to change things. In fact, Rowling ends up keeping only a third of her ideas in that "Plot" column for Chapter 13. Here's how the column would look if you were to strike through what Rowling decides to leave out altogether, italicize what she moves to another chapter, and put in bold what she keeps in the final version of the chapter:

Harry has a lesson scheduled with Snape ~~but he skips it~~ . . . **[Harry goes] to Hogsmeade with Ron and**

> **Hermione.** ~~They meet Lupin and Tonks but can't talk because Umbridge is tailing them, so they pass a note.~~ **Harry, Ron, and Hermione are recruiting for Dumbledore's Army.** *Hagrid has fresh injuries.*

This example reinforces my opening statement in the Introduction that, if you find your 99 scenes and put them in the right order, you will be all set. The majority of the changes that Rowling makes between this grid and her final draft is simply rearranging. By using a tool like the series grid, you won't necessarily get your entire order right on the first try, but during your next draft, if a scene is out of place, it will be vastly more obvious than it was in your previous draft. It will practically walk up to you and, while not being able to speak, gesture somewhat impatiently as to where it should go.

The Key Scene

The key scene is where multiple series collide (I'm getting used to the new lingo!) and send the story spinning off in new directions. These occasions, when series come together in a proximate, physical, literal sense, give readers the feeling that "it is all coming together." And that emotional pay-off is what keeps readers reading. When readers describe a book as "slow," saying that "nothing happens," it is due to a lack of interactions between series.

The true blessing of a spatial outline such as the series grid is how it allows you to see the way series collide with each other or how they don't. In Rowling's outline, all of her series intersect and interact with each other in such a way that, if one were taken out, the story would be off-kilter. This is especially powerful in the key scene that is included on her handwritten outline in the fourth row, labeled Chapter 16 and titled "Black Marks."* In this chapter, Harry

---

* In the published version, this is Chapter 22, "St. Mungo's Hospital for Magical Maladies and Injuries."

is desperately trying to explain to his professors and friends that, while he was sleeping, he had a vision of Voldemort's snake attacking Mr. Weasley.

In this key scene, which is also the midpoint of the novel, as we will see in a minute, Rowling brings together four of the six series from her grid:

1. *Hall of Prophecy:* It's the place where the snake attacks Mr. Weasley.

2. *Cho/Ginny:* Harry has to watch Ginny Weasley and her siblings be told about their father's injuries.

3. *Order of the Phoenix:* Mr. Weasley is attacked while on duty for the Order.

4. *Dumbledore's Army:* The Weasley children comprise a significant number of the D.A., and this attack on their father drives them to work even harder in the group.

Rowling acknowledges in her series grid that she's trying to push together these four series to create a key scene. I have said before that the strength of a novel is based upon the strength of its key scenes. Whether these key scenes need to occur at the intervals prescribed by a formula, I will leave up to you.

What of This Midpoint Business?

In the Introduction, I reproduced in brief the formula currently in vogue for crafting a narrative. One of the champions of this formula defines the midpoint as "a big fat unexpected twist" that "empowers the hero in the transition from Part 2 wanderer to Part 3 warrior."[*] Maybe that does work; it works here. In the very chapter we were

---

[*]   Larry Brooks, *Story Engineering* (Cincinnati: Writer's Digest Books, 2011), 193.

just studying, Harry is forced to take action, to transition from a "wanderer" to a "warrior."

You can use the three tools of Book Architecture—the series target, the series arc, and the series grid—to perfect a formula, or you can use what you are learning to plot and outline without using a formula, creating instead a design that is original and authentic to your work. Or you could choose an option that is beyond both of these dualities, which is what Joseph Heller did in his novel *Catch-22*. He used the series grid to create an exploding midpoint, the effects of which are felt throughout the entire book. For more about that, you'll have to turn the page.

Getting Hands-on:

Take your series that have proven relevant to your theme and create an expanded series grid. You can do this digitally in a spreadsheet or on a very large piece of paper.

Set up the rows by scene or chapter or whatever distinction allows you to easily distinguish one set of manuscript pages from another. In the first columns, you can put your central series and any relevant time stamps that will help readers keep track of where they are. After that, flesh out the rest of the columns with your series, such as objects, locations, phrases, and flat and round characters.

Chapter Six

The Entire Series Grid in Joseph Heller's Novel *Catch-22*

Our work on the series grid comes to its apex with Joseph Heller's recovered outline from his creation of the novel *Catch-22*. We don't know that he called it an outline; we're going to call it a series grid because that's exactly what it is. It almost takes your breath away. Some writers will throw up their hands when they view the next page and say that it looks too complicated. One friend told me that it looked too much like an accounting ledger. Other writers will be fascinated and want to study the full-sized transcription available on BookArchitecture.com and know what every part of it does while they read the book closely.

You may be in the middle like me. What helped me process the document that follows was the knowledge that Heller was, like his main character, Yossarian, a bombardier in World War II. They took care of their maps in those days before GPS, and this is really just so the author could hit his targets.

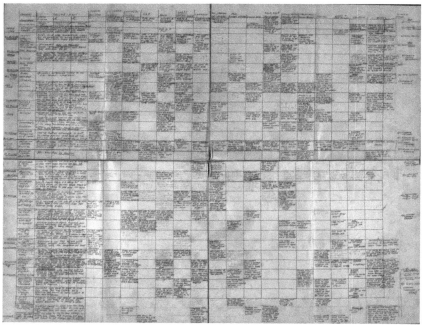

Image used courtesy of Robert D. Farber University Archives &
Special Collections Department, Brandeis University

I'm not expecting you to be able to read this image, by the way. That's what the transcription is for. I just like to look at it. I had the good fortune of seeing the original at the Brandeis University library: it is four pieces of posterboard held together by heavy tape. Heller did it in pencil, and there is smudging and erasing all over the place because the series grid is a tool—concepts change as we complete them.

Even from this distance, we can see there are a lot of empty boxes. This indicates that within each series column there are iterations, but then there are long gaps of time in which that series is not used, creating foreshadowing and suspense. We can also see that not all of Heller's series start at the same time, and some end before the others do. This is all part of the richness of the texture of both the grid and the narrative that it helped support. If you were one of those people who objected to the series grid at the beginning of this book, likening it to an assignment from junior high, you probably did so because you thought your work was too complex for such a simple chart. Fair point, but, really, you just need a more complex chart.

In a work as sprawling as *Catch-22*, Heller needed some way of keeping track of when and how the events were supposed to happen, especially because he was going where few novelists of the time had gone in terms of presenting events in narrative order, as opposed to strict chronological order. (Important note: even though the novel is presented in narrative order, this series grid is in chronological order.) Having this map actually helped Heller's imagination. In an interview with *The Paris Review,* he said:

> "There's an essay of T. S. Eliot's in which he praises the disciplines of writing, claiming that if one is forced to write within a certain framework, the imagination is taxed to its utmost and will produce its richest ideas. Given total freedom, however, the chances are good that the work will sprawl."[*]

It's something you have heard me say before: intelligent planning is not the enemy of creative genius.

The Central Series in *Catch-22*

In Columns 1 and 2, we have Heller's central series. I'm really not making this up. There are other items listed in these columns—for instance, historical tidbits such as "Allies Enter Rome"—but these are really just notes for the author to remember the historical backdrop against which his events take place—none of these actually appear in the book. Some dates also appear: "Thanksgiving Day," "December

---

[*] Joseph Heller, "The Art of Fiction." *Paris Review* 60 (Winter 1974).

1944," but neither these time stamps nor the chronology of the war are how the reader makes his or her way through the book.

Instead, it is the *Number of Missions* that Yossarian has flown that leads the readers through the narrative. Each officer in Yossarian's squadron, located on a fictitious island in the Mediterranean, must fly a certain number of missions before they are eligible to be rotated home. The central series of the novel depicts how the number of missions required stretches from twenty-five to beyond eighty at the hands of the sadistically stupid Colonel Cathcart, and how the number of missions Yossarian has flown is always heartbreakingly, frustratingly just less than the number required.

CATCH–22:
COLUMNS I AND 2

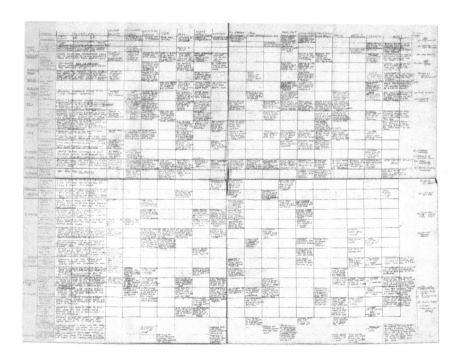

Even in a fictional universe that verges on chaos, we can keep track of the number of missions Yossarian has flown. In fact, because this central series is so strong it allows us to jump around to any row, meaning any month in the year 1944, and know where we are relative to where we just were.

Because Heller presents the events of *Catch-22* in narrative order, he does not begin with Yossarian enlisting or flying his first mission. Rather, the book begins with Yossarian in the battlefield hospital faking a liver ailment. His close friend, Clevinger, has just died. Yossarian finds out that the number of missions needed for release is only forty, even as that information is contradicted by others.

> "Then I can go home, right? I've got forty-eight."
>
> "No, you can't go home," ex-P.F.C. Wintergreen corrected him. "Are you crazy or something?"
>
> "Why not?"
>
> "Catch-22."
>
> "Catch-22?" Yossarian was stunned. "What the hell has Catch-22 got to do with it?"
>
> "Catch-22," Doc Daneeka answered patiently [. . .] "says you've always got to do what your commanding officer tells you to. [. . .] regulations do say you have to obey every order. That's the catch. Even if the colonel were disobeying a Twenty-seventh Air Force order by making you fly more missions, you'd still have to fly them, or you'd be guilty of disobeying an order of his. And then Twenty-seventh Air Force Headquarters would really jump on you."
>
> Yossarian slumped with disappointment. "Then I really have to fly the fifty missions, don't I?" he grieved.
>
> "The fifty-five," Doc Daneeka corrected him.
>
> "What fifty-five?"

> "The fifty-five missions the colonel now wants
> all of you to fly."   (p. 58)

In the above passage, the strong central series also serves the theme of *Catch-22*, which Heller has confided twice to the novel's pages:

> "There just doesn't seem to be any logic to this system of rewards and punishment."   (p. 170)

> "Immoral logic seemed to be confounding him at every turn."   (p. 387)

In Chapter Four, I advocated for the value of being able to sum up one's work in a sentence. And for the most part, when we do that, we can't resist putting that statement in the book itself. Knowing your theme isn't the end of the job, of course—it's actually only the beginning. Joe Heller, as his friends called him, didn't necessarily agree that having a message was the objective of a novel. "In fact," he said in the same *Paris Review* interview, "any 'message' becomes part of the texture, stirred so much that it's as negligible as a teaspoon of salt in a large stew."

But imagine that stew without any salt . . .

In this stew, the theme of "immoral logic" is told to us only twice; the rest of the time it is shown as it animates the series of *Catch-22*. Yossarian tries to get his friend Orr grounded from flying any more missions by convincing Doc Daneeka to do so on the basis of Orr's mental health.

> "Is Orr crazy?"
> "He sure is," Doc Daneeka said.
> "Can you ground him?"
> "I sure can. But first he has to ask me to. That's part
>   of the rule."

"Then why doesn't he ask you to?"

"Because he's crazy," Doc Daneeka said. "He has to be crazy to keep flying combat missions after all the close calls he's had. Sure, I can ground Orr. But first he has to ask me to."

"That's all he has to do to be grounded?"

"That's all. Let him ask me."

"And then you can ground him?" Yossarian asked.

"No. Then I can't ground him."

"You mean there's a catch?"

"Sure there's a catch," Doc Daneeka replied. "Catch-22. Anyone who wants to get out of combat duty isn't really crazy."

. . .Yossarian was moved very deeply by the absolute simplicity of this clause of Catch-22 and let out a respectful whistle.

"That's some catch, that Catch-22," he observed.

"It's the best there is," Doc Daneeka agreed.   (p. 46)

Meanwhile, back at the base, the missions have been raised to sixty by Colonel Cathcart in an effort to get *The Saturday Evening Post* to feature his bomber group in a photoshoot. The immoral logic of rewards and punishment grows even darker when the pilot McWatt, messing around on the base, comes too close to the new enlist, Kid Sampson, and chops him in half on a swimming dock. Destroyed by what he has done, McWatt dips his wings in salute to Yossarian and others on the beach before intentionally crashing his plane into the side of a mountain. Cathcart's reaction to Kid Sampson's grisly death and McWatt's ensuing suicide is to raise the number of missions required to sixty-five.

There are many other notable iterations in the central series, from Cathcart's power-hungry rant that perhaps the number of missions isn't yet high enough and "he ought to increase the number at once to seventy, eighty, a hundred, or even two hundred, three hundred, or six thousand!" (p. 214), to the realization that Cathcart himself has flown only four missions (and his coconspirator Milo Minderbinder only five), to the climactic moment when Yossarian refuses to fly any more missions. The central character has been changed conclusively by the central series, thus hastening the end of the novel.

The Other Columns in Heller's Series Grid

If the vertical element of Heller's series grid is arranged chronologically, with emphasis on the central series of the number of missions that Yossarian has flown, how is it arranged horizontally? What is across the top row?

CATCH–22:
ROW 1

For the most part, Heller lists his characters here, but not always. Column 21, for example, is labeled "Casualties." It is an axiom of series work that, if you want to get your reader to notice something, you have to repeat it. If you really, really want to get your reader to notice something, such as how unimaginably brutal war actually is, you repeat it seventeen times, which is the number of main characters who die in *Catch-22*.

Once we can identify *Casualties* as a series while we are reading, the variations come fast and furious. The soldier who sees everything twice dies of some mysterious disease. The soldier in white is pronounced dead at the hospital. Snowden freezes to death "in sunlight," McWatt accidentally cuts Kid Sampson in half with his airplane, and then kills himself. Dunbar is "disappeared," the maid is murdered by Aarfy, and Nately and Dobbs are killed in a mid-air crash. Clevinger is never seen again. The repetitions exist just so no one misses the point. By the end of this very funny book, readers may themselves feel a little sick and heavy, like things are not really that funny.

Most of the rest of the columns are labeled with character names. A round character like Yossarian, who undergoes a complex change, has three columns to himself (3–5), while flat characters either have one column or are doubled up in the same column because they share the same function, such as Doc Daneeka and Dr. Stubbs in Column 13 and Colonel Cathcart and Colonel Korn in Column 17. Using the series grid can help you track whether your round characters are evolving (or devolving), or how relationships are faring as we see those characters consistently appear in the same row on the grid.

A Round Character Has Several Series

As a round character, Yossarian has several series by which we can identify the changes he is going through. This is why I like using the word "series" as it applies to character better than characterization. Heller has some characterization scrawled into his grid: Yossarian is "Urban," and "Assyrian," but that doesn't really tell us anything about his character. Or, rather, that is *all* it does: tell us.

Yossarian's character is *shown* by the series that represent him to us. We know his relative seniority by the central series of the *Number of Missions* he has flown. We know whether Yossarian is in favor with his higher-ups by his *Rank*, which shifts from lead bombardier to wing bombardier, then getting reinstated as lead, then getting demoted again. But nowhere do we get to know where Yossarian is at better than through the *Naked* series.

The first iteration of the *Naked* series occurs when Yossarian is treating Snowden's eventually fatal wound; Yossarian strips down to help the tail-gunner who keeps complaining, "I'm cold."

But then Yossarian leaves his clothes off. He goes to Snowden's funeral naked and escapes notice by climbing a nearby tree. Yossarian is still naked in the third iteration of the series when he lines up to get his medal for the mission over Ferrara. His superiors try to explain to the General that a man was killed in Yossarian's plane over Avignon the previous week and bled all over him, and that Yossarian is naked because his uniform hasn't come back from the laundry yet, that his other uniforms are in the laundry, and so is all his underwear.

> "That sounds like a lot of crap to me," General
>   Dreedle declared.
> "It is a lot of crap, sir," Yossarian said.   (p. 218)

The *Naked* series shows us a man at his breaking point better than a long discussion of a breaking point ever could. These effects are intended, but don't take my word for it. Here is a close-up of the grid (Columns 3-5, Row N) where we can read Heller's own listing of the *Naked* series. If those aren't series iterations, I don't know what is.

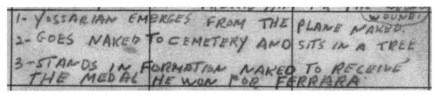

Image used courtesy of Robert D. Farber University Archives &
Special Collections Department, Brandeis University

A Flat Character Has One Series

A good example of a flat character with only one series is Snowden, the new tail-gunner, whom no one has really met; he shows up for his first mission only to get severely wounded on his first flight. Snowden (alive) appears in only one scene, but because Heller uses narrative order as opposed to chronological order to present his events, he can revisit that same scene four times over the course of the book as more of what transpires there is progressively revealed.

In the first iteration, we get just two lines of dialogue after Snowden has been hit by enemy anti-aircraft fire:

> "I'm cold," Snowden had whimpered. "I'm cold."
> "There, there," Yossarian had tried to comfort him.
>   "There, there."   (p. 166)

In the second iteration, we learn a little bit more about the scene. It occurs on a mission to Avignon. Instead of enjoying a "milk run" (slang for an easy flight, such as going to pick up milk), their bomber encounters intense resistance: they are hit, they speed down recklessly, bodies dangling weightless inside the plane, until the pilot,

Huple, levels out the plane again. But there is far more to cope with than just regaining control of the flight, because now they must climb again through enemy fire to reach their escape, and some irretrievable damage has been done.

> Dobbs was weeping when Yossarian jammed his jack plug back into the intercom system and was able to hear again.
> "Help him, help him," Dobbs was sobbing. "Help him, help him."
> "Help who? Help who?" Yossarian called back. "Help who?"
> "The bombardier, the bombardier," Dobbs cried. "He doesn't answer. Help the bombardier, help the bombardier."
> "I'm the bombardier," Yossarian cried back at him. "I'm the bombardier. I'm all right. I'm all right."
> "Then help him, help him," Dobbs wept. "Help him, help him."
> "Help who? Help who?"
> "The radio-gunner," Dobbs begged. "Help the radio-gunner."
> "I'm cold," Snowden whimpered feebly over the intercom system then in a bleat of plaintive agony. "Please help me. I'm cold."   (p. 225–26)

In this third iteration, we learn that Yossarian does indeed try to help Snowden by leaving the bomb bay and wriggling to the back of the plane. There, Yossarian takes apart the first-aid kit and treats Snowden for a "yawning, raw, melon-shaped hole as big as a football in the outside of his thigh, the unsevered, blood-soaked muscle fibers inside pulsating weirdly like blind things with lives of their own [. . .]" (p. 331–32)

Sorry for the graphic description. War is hell. It gives Yossarian post-traumatic stress disorder, which becomes progressively more intense as the novel wears on and he devolves into marching everywhere backward with his gun on his hip, continuously spinning around to make sure no one is sneaking up on him from behind. We don't have to wonder forever about what caused this PTSD; in the second-to-last chapter, the final Snowden iteration is revealed.

We know Snowden is cold; we know Yossarian is reassuring him with a grin that he will be all right. But Yossarian is treating him for the wrong wound—a devastating leg injury to be sure but nothing compared to the wound Yossarian sees now. A three-inch chunk of flak has blasted through the center of Snowden's body, making his death an absolute certainty. I will spare you the horror of what Yossarian witnesses then; perhaps you have already read it or will. The unforgettable scene concludes:

> "I'm cold," Snowden said. "I'm cold."
> "There, there," said Yossarian. "There, there."
> He pulled the rip cord of Snowden's parachute and covered his body with the white nylon sheets.
> "I'm cold."
> "There, there."   (p. 440)

The repetitions and variations of the *Snowden* series are masterful—and yes, I do refer to him as a "series" and not as a "character." No one knows anything about him! The repetition occurs in presenting the same scene four times, the variation occurs in the expanding word count for each iteration: from 44 words to 540 words, back a little to 308 words, and then onto the climactic iteration of 1,792 words.

CATCH-22:
SNOWDEN

In the above image, I have highlighted the three rows (M, N, and P) where Snowden appears. Remember, this chart was done in chronological order, but Heller presents his material in narrative order.* In other words, the events in Rows M, N, and P all happen in July 1944, either on the mission over Avignon or shortly thereafter. In terms of the reading experience, however, Heller spreads the four iterations of the Snowden series across a wide swath of the book: from p. 166, to p. 226, to p. 331, to p. 437. Once that second iteration comes along, showing us that *this is going to mean something*, the long gaps between iterations provide suspense.

---

* You may ask, "How can we tell which scenes appear where in the narrative compared to the grid?" The answer is, you can't. You just have to read the book.

Chronologically speaking, Snowden's scene occurs—wait for it—at the midpoint of the book. Heller's genius is that he has taken the midpoint—you know, where the main character goes from "wanderer" to "warrior," or where, in this case, Yossarian goes from "unthinking warrior" to "ex-warrior"—and spread it throughout the book. The midpoint in this sense is always happening, and that contributes to the sense of both literal and figurative bombs exploding everywhere. If there were a formula to demonstrate how to create a novel in 3-D like this, it would have to be one of those physics formulas that covers multiple blackboards and gives you a headache just looking at it. Instead of resorting to a formula, however complex, we can use the series grid to develop strong series such as the central series of the *Number of Missions*, a telling round character series such as Yossarian getting and staying *Naked*, and a heartbreakingly simple flat character series such as *Snowden*. If we do that, our readers will have enough familiarity with what is happening that we can take even greater chances.

Use of the Series Grid

Hopefully, by now Heller's series grid is looking a little less scary. I can imagine making one for my secret memoir project due out in 2027 and using it to establish where series initiate, recapitulate, connect—where they collide! By populating such a grid, I could see which chapters have too much going on and which series have to be cut back or cut loose. I could use it to make sure my series are introduced in a way that makes sense, are used enough, and in the right way, because if they are important enough to be included, I should at least do them justice.

I can imagine such a series grid will also help because I don't plan to quit my day job as editor and ghostwriter to complete my memoir. Rather, it will take me several years because it already has (not that I've been working on it the whole time—I stopped to write *this* book).

The question then becomes: Should you get rid of your series grid at the end? I mean, thank God that Heller didn't. It offers the rarest glimpse into the construction of a complex narrative. But it also includes notes Heller would never have put in the book in their current form, such as: "Nately's Whore becomes a symbol of [Yossarian's] guilt and responsibility for never intervening in the injustices he knows exist everywhere." Okay, so maybe we didn't need to know *that*; that's stating things a little baldly. Disposing of one's notes is what the Czech author Milan Kundera meant when he said that an author was obligated to clean up after himself or herself.

Another Czech author, Franz Kafka, took this to the logical extreme by requesting that his friend and literary executor, Max Brod, burn all of his unpublished works unread: novel fragments, illustrations, one-page aphorisms, all of it. There are many reasons we are fortunate that Brod refused this difficult last request, with just one of them being that it would have made the next chapter much less interesting.

Getting Hands-on:

Complete your series grid as far as you can at this point in your drafting process. Pay special attention to the gaps between iterations in a series: Are you building on what you have created? Are you expecting your reader to remember too much, for too long?

You can refer to your series grid while you are writing a particular scene or chapter to determine when to feature something and how hard to hit it. You can also use it to take your foot off the gas pedal at times, remembering that there is only so much that can you get across at a given time.

Finally, you can erase things—iterations, or even entire series, that don't work—as you get increasingly comfortable with your theme.

Chapter Seven

Making Series Grids and Series Arcs with Franz Kafka's Novella *The Metamorphosis*

Y ou may not ever read Franz Kafka's novella, *The Metamorphosis,** or perhaps you already have. To each her or his own. But what you should do at some point in your writing career is take your favorite work of literature apart using the tools we have developed here. When I was in graduate school with the poet Robert Bly, he told us that, after reading various styles and trying to imitate them, you should eventually apprentice yourself to a master. You will likely choose somebody other than Kafka, and you will have to choose something other than this novella, because I have done the work for us here. Whichever narrative you pick, my advice is to read it slowly and draw up its series grid, along with a few series arcs thrown in to boot. In this chapter, we will discuss why you don't have to draw an arc for every series, although you certainly

---

* I am using the edition translated by Susan Bernofsky (New York: Norton, 2014).

can. This journey of discovery is how we learn. I have chosen *The Metamorphosis* for a number of reasons, most of them deeply psychological. Also, the book in your hands was published on the 100th anniversary of the publication of Kafka's gem, so consider this my very modest contribution to the reams of scholarship on this story.

Creating a Series Grid from Scratch

I am first going to create a series grid of Kafka's novella from scratch; you can see the full transcription at the end of this chapter. I also put together a kind of low-fi photoessay so you can see that I don't necessarily have superior tools or insight before I get started on something like this. That's why we do it in pencil initially.

FIRST WE BUY A BIG PIECE OF PAPER

KAFKA BROKE THE STORY INTO THIRDS SO WE SHOULD TOO

KEEPING TRACK BY BATCHES OF 7 PAGES

While doing this, I couldn't help but be reminded of some of my favorite Kafka quotes. Because I serve on the Library Foundation's board of directors in my town, I was allowed to choose a quote to engrave on a brick for the grounds of our new library. I really wanted to pick: "There is hope, yes, but not for us." – Franz Kafka. I was encouraged to think the better of it, and chose instead a poem by the Japanese Zen monk Ryokan: "Ever since I saw the light/I have set at naught the worldly glories/leaving my destiny to chance."* I bring up this particular quote of Kafka's just so we don't water down where he was really coming from, you know?

SOME SERIES   SHOULD WE GO OUT, OR DOWN?   MORE SERIES

You may already know from Action Step #5 in *BYB* (where I advise printing out your manuscript at least once during the revision process and slicing it into its component scenes) that I recommend hands-on work. Having your hands into the material by constructing this kind of chart helps us get deeper into the choices that were made to bring about the story. Because choices certainly were made.

---

* The second runner-up was by Lars Gustafsson from *A Tiler's Afternoon*: "It was really amazing the way some people could drink."

THAT'S IT!   BUT WE HAVE MORE PAPER...   WELL THEN LET'S CUT IT!

Setting Up the Rows: Kafka's Scenes

When we are setting up the rows, the easiest way to keep track at first is by noting the divisions the author has given us. In this case, the novella is divided into three parts. It is tempting to dip into the mountain of Kafka criticism and start relating constructs like those suggested by Heinz Politzer: Part I describes the main character, Gregor Samsa, in relationship to his profession, Part II in relationship to his family, and Part III in relationship to himself.* But let's not. That might be true, but let's resolve to draw our conclusions from the series grid itself.

In this case, I think it is easiest to create the individual rows on the grid by simply dividing the story into batches of about seven pages each. In Bernofsky's translation, the story is 98 pages long, so that's 15 rows (p. 21–27, where the novella starts, is Row 1, p. 28–34 is Row 2, etc.). Kafka weighted each of his three parts almost exactly the same; each is between 31 and 34 pages long. Therefore, in the transcription, each part takes up five rows.

I could have broken up the story by scene, and next I'll give you my thoughts on where the scenes of the novella are divided. But

---

* Heinz Politzer, *Franz Kafka: Parable and Paradox* (Cornell University Press, 1966), 65.

you can also take my word for it that breaking this narrative up by page numbers simplifies what can be a pretty dense process, and skip to the next subhead, "Setting Up the Columns: Kafka's Series." (You can also keep reading this subhead if you'd like a somewhat impressionistic synopsis of the story.)

I'm seeing eight scenes in this novella. Scene One starts at the beginning, p. 21, where Gregor has been transformed into a "monstrous insect," and continues until the middle of p. 31, when someone rings the doorbell. Uh oh! Scene Two is marked by the arrival of Gregor's General Manager from his office, inquiring about Gregor's lateness. This scene has a climax: tired of being characterized as stubborn or lazy, Gregor as the monstrous insect manages to get out of bed and open his bedroom door with his bug jaws. What happens next is that the General Manager, along with Gregor's father, mother, and sister, sees Gregor . . . and that changes everything. Scene Two concludes with the end of Part I on p. 51.

Scene Three starts with the beginning of Part II, and its main action is Gregor's sister, Grete, trying to figure out what to feed Gregor in his current state. His favorite drink used to be milk, but now all he really likes is old cheese. After the foodstuffs section, I believe Scene Three ends on p. 59, when we move on from actions that take place on a specific day in a specific place, and we enter a summary highlighted by representative actions: symbolic events that are repeated over a period of time. Scene Four starts with representative actions—"This was how Gregor now received his food each day"—and that is all it really contains. Additional examples include: "[. . .] he was sometimes able to overhear this or that [. . .]" and "[. . .] sometimes general exhaustion made it impossible for him to go on listening[. . . .]" Such representative actions speed up time by recounting events with a broader brush; when that style ends on p. 70, Scene Four ends. Scene Five starts by taking us out of representative actions and putting us into a distinct action: "Gregor's wish to see his mother was soon fulfilled." Now we've got specific, rather than representative, actions: people hiding, fainting, yelling, and eventually throwing dangerous missiles of fruit at Gregor's body. Scene Five ends with the conclusion of Part II.

Scene Six starts at the beginning of Part III: "The grievous wound Gregor had received, which plagued him for over a month" and contains only representative actions. As with the transition between Scenes Four and Five, the transition between Scenes Six and Seven occurs when a general description of affairs ends and gives way to one distinct time when an action will occur: "On this very evening [. . .]" (p. 98). Scene Seven ends when he dies. Sad face. Scene Eight starts from there (p. 110) and runs from his cursory funeral until the end of the novella.

Setting Up the Columns: Kafka's Series

Okay, so setting up the rows either by batches of pages or scenes—that was the easy part. How do we divide the columns? How do we choose our series? We could follow Heller, and space out the top row largely by characters: Gregor; Gregor's sister, Grete; Gregor's father, etc. Or we could just go pure series and simply keep track of what repeats, paying special attention to the elements that repeat the most and/or that repeat when other series do, i.e., in key scenes and other critical moments.

In the first two columns, let's put the two central series of the novella: *Will Gregor Get to Work?* and *Gregor's Decomposition.* Did I say *two* central series? Yes, there are two central series, although not two at a time; the first gives way to the second, as we will see. This does not necessarily make the novella about more than one thing; because the two central series are sequential, it is more of an *innovation* that follows the rules of the central series rather than a violation.

Let's recall for a minute the criteria for a central series. We need something that helps us keep track of time. All series have to answer a question (because when all the questions are answered, the story is over), but the central series answers the most visceral or immediate questions. Like, *Will Gregor Get to Work?* The four major iterations of this first central series are as follows:

THE METAMORPHOSIS:
SERIES GRID 1

ITERATION NUMBER	PAGE NUMBER	SERIES NAME: WILL GREGOR GET TO WORK? SERIES TYPE: CENTRAL (NUMBER 1)
1	24–25	SEES ALARM CLOCK, CAN'T MOVE, GOING TO MISS THE TRAIN
2	30	IF HE DOESN'T GET OUT OF BED, SOMEONE FROM THE OFFICE WILL COME CHECK ON HIM
3	35	CAN'T GET UP TO GREET GENERAL MANAGER
4	42	OPENS LOCK WITH HIS OWN JAWS

After the fourth iteration, the General Manager, who has seen Gregor as a bug, runs out onto the landing of the Samsa's apartment building, uttering a loud "Oh!" that sounds like the wind howling, as he leaps down several steps at once and vanishes. Guess we're not going to work now.

When the first central series concludes—the question is answered—the second central series begins immediately in the same row (p. 35–41): Gregor's father, who, up until this point, has been relatively composed, seizes a walking stick in one hand and a newspaper in another. Driving Gregor backward into his room, Gregor's father eventually shoves his son so strongly that it causes Gregor to bleed profusely. This spurs on *Gregor's Decomposition*, which has the following major iterations:

THE METAMORPHOSIS:
SERIES GRID 2

ITERATION NUMBER	PAGE NUMBER	SERIES NAME: GREGOR'S DECOMPOSITION SERIES TYPE: CENTRAL (NUMBER 2)
1	41	INJURES HIMSELF, BROWN FLUID RUNS OUT
2	51	SCRAPES HIMSELF ON DOOR, FATHER SHOVES HIM IN, BLEEDING PROFUSELY
3	53	LEFT SIDE LIKE ONE LONG CONTRACTING SCAR, LIMPING OUTRIGHT
4	58	WOUNDS HAVE HEALED?
5	60	EATING SLOWS DOWN
6	67	LOSING HIS EYESIGHT
7	79	ENGULFED BY CORROSIVE MEDICINE, HIT BY SHARDS OF GLASS
8	84	GETS APPLE HURLED BY HIS FATHER EMBEDDED IN HIS BACK
9	85–86	WOUND BECOMES GRIEVOUS; HOBBLES LIKE AN INVALID
10	95	STOPS EATING; HOLDS FOOD IN HIS MOUTH ONLY TO SPIT IT OUT AGAIN
11	108	SMALL DISTANCES HE TRAVELS BECOME IMPOSSIBLY GREAT
12	109	NO LONGER CAPABLE OF MOVING AT ALL
13	110	DIES

I have drawn the arc of this series below. I did not draw the arc of the first central series because, to me, it is over too soon. You can certainly draw the arcs of all of your series as I've mentioned, or you can home in on the ones that are giving you the most trouble, as a client of mine, Tye, does in the conclusion to this book. Or, you can draw the arcs of the most relevant series, which you ascertained after putting your series sentences in a top-down order of importance in Chapter Four. That is what I have done in this chapter; I drew four arcs of the nine series that I ended up putting into the grid. I felt the relative improvement or deterioration of each iteration along the vertical axis while carefully noting the page number where it occurs on the horizontal axis. The series arc for *Gregor's Decomposition* looks like the following:

THE METAMORPHOSIS:
SERIES ARC I

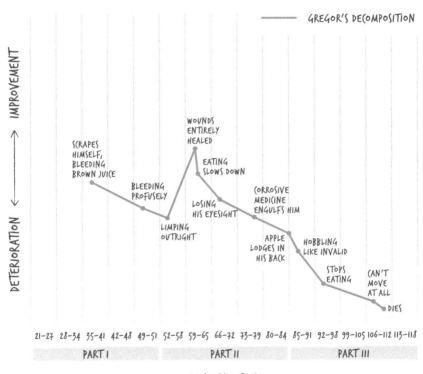

That's a pretty Kafkaesque looking arc. There is hope, yes, but not for us. A couple of interesting aspects; first, even this arc has an upside to it, when Gregor's wounds seem to have entirely healed on

p. 58. In order for such a development to be believable—it is, after all, a sharp rise in a fairly few number of pages—it helps if the reader needs that reprieve emotionally, which we do. The other observation we can make is that the *Gregor's Decomposition* series achieves its suspense not by an absence of information, but rather by a steady stream of iterations: what you may have heard called in writing circles the "IV drip of information," or "dropping the bread crumbs to lead readers where you want them to go."* The suspense here is derived not so much from what will happen, as this arc really goes in only one direction, but from how unremittingly insensitive his family members become to his plight. Good stuff.

Columns Three and Four in the Series Grid

In the third column, I have charted a series entitled *Job Security*. In some ways, this series is the natural extension of *Will Gregor Get to Work?* because it lets us know what will happen if Gregor *doesn't* get to work. It's tempting to go for something bigger than *Job Security*, something like *Hierarchy*, or even *The Individual and the Collective*, but hold on. One of the best things about this story is that Kafka doesn't tell us about things very often, rather, he *shows* us things. Gregor hasn't been ill once in five years, yet the first day he is even a few minutes late, the General Manager shows up at his door. That doesn't bode well. Furthermore, it comes out that Gregor's productivity of late has been highly unsatisfactory. And then there is the matter of the cash payments that have been recently entrusted into Gregor's care. . . .

All of this adds up to the reader's realization that Gregor's "position is anything but secure." (p. 37) Why is this such a big deal? Because if Gregor loses his position in the firm, he will also lose his position in his family. He works there only because his parents

---

* A reference to the fairy tale "Hansel and Gretel."

owe the company an "ancient debt." Gregor had not intended to be in this job for life—another five or six years at most. "He felt great pride at having been able to give his parents and sister a life like this in such a beautiful apartment. But what if all this tranquility, all this prosperity and contentment were now coming to a horrific end?" (p. 54)

I have put the series about Gregor's *Family's Fortune* in Column Four. I have also chosen to chart the *Family's Fortune* series arc; I took my cue as to the importance of this series from the fact that there are so many iterations:

THE METAMORPHOSIS:
SERIES ARC 2

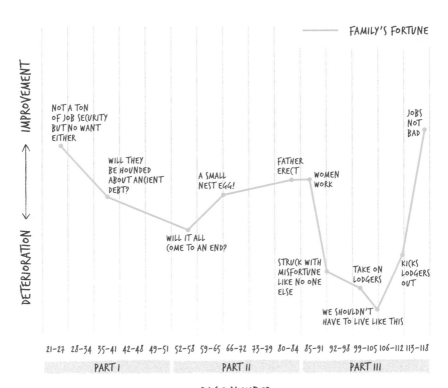

The *Family's Fortune* arc heads up for the first time on p. 65 when, it turns out, Gregor's family is not completely unfortunate; Gregor's father has managed to preserve a small nest egg, "really only a tiny one," that Gregor knew nothing about. Gregor is being used. With the money his father held onto, the Samsa family could have paid off their debt sooner, allowing Gregor free to leave his job. Kafka's irony is at its thickest when Gregor nods behind his door when he hears of this news, "delighted at this unexpected prudence and thrift."

So Gregor's family are all going to have to find work, not a bad thing in itself. His father has found a job as a porter and is now "standing properly erect; dressed in a smart blue uniform with gold buttons." (p. 83) His mother sews ladies' underthings for a dress shop, while his sister has taken a job as a salesgirl.

In the end, none of this is enough. Because they can't move to a new apartment with Gregor as he is, they have been "struck with a misfortune such as no one else in their entire circle of relations and friends had ever experienced." (p. 90) That's nearly hitting rock bottom, but the arc dips even lower when they are forced to take on three lodgers, solemn bearded gentlemen with more than a touch of OCD. The *Family's Fortune* series arc doesn't start heading back up for good until after Gregor dies. When that happens, the Samsa family is no longer powerless: Gregor's father orders the lodgers out of his home, and it turns out their jobs aren't really that bad. They even decide to all take the day off!

This kind of contingency, where one series depends on another, is a great reason to draw two series arcs on the same graph. When we plot the *Family's Fortune* series arc against the arc of *Gregor's Decomposition*, we can see that he has their fate pretty much in his hands . . . until he doesn't, and their fortunes take off:

THE METAMORPHOSIS:
SERIES ARC 3

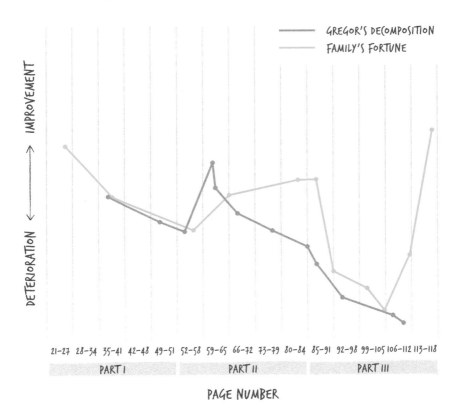

Family's Fortune and Gregor's Decomposition are what might be called a series twin. Their iterations are continually linked together, something you can see by filling out a series grid. These co-incidences cause the material in each series to interact and intersect—and yes, collide. In this case, one series ends in one direction, while conclusively pushing the other series in another direction. This process itself generates meaning, as we will see shortly.

Flat Characters and Round Characters: Columns Five and Six

The next two columns on our series grid deal with two characters: one flat and one round. Gregor's father is a flat character because all he ever really does is get mad. When he gets mad, he gets violent, and this occurs at the end of both Part I (when Gregor's father backs him into his room brandishing a walking stick), and Part II (when the apple that Gregor's father has launched lands in Gregor's back and turns into a grievous wound).

The *Gregor and Grete* series, on the other hand, shows Gregor's sister going through a change and thus becoming a round character. When Gregor first turns into a monstrous insect, Grete is the only one to approach his condition with a lament. Later, when Gregor finds himself unable to explain himself suitably to his General Manager, he wishes Grete were there because she is clever and could have talked the man out of his fear. She is the only family member who cares for Gregor, bringing him milk, which used to be his favorite drink, except now he prefers two-day-old milk and old cheese, so she brings him that instead. She moves the armchair back to where she knows he likes it after she is done cleaning his room.

She's really doing the best she can, until Gregor interferes with her plan to adjust the contents of his room one time too many for his liking. Gregor's mother, who hasn't seen him in weeks, is part of the moving team until Gregor bursts out of hiding. His mother faints, which enrages Grete; Grete then raises her fist at Gregor with "a threatening glower." Her gesture of violence, along with shouting his name—the first time she has addressed him directly since his metamorphosis—shows her allegiance transferring to the side of their father.

Something happens, something changes, represented by a very steep downward arc in the middle of the novella. The depth of this change is why I chose to draw a series arc for *Gregor and Grete* and not for his *Father's Violence*.

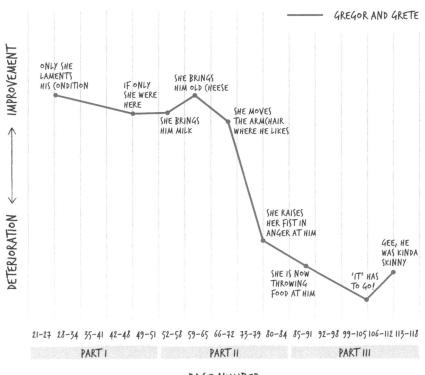

THE METAMORPHOSIS:
SERIES ARC 4

——— GREGOR AND GRETE

IMPROVEMENT

DETERIORATION

ONLY SHE LAMENTS HIS CONDITION

IF ONLY SHE WERE HERE

SHE BRINGS HIM OLD CHEESE

SHE BRINGS HIM MILK

SHE MOVES THE ARMCHAIR WHERE HE LIKES

SHE RAISES HER FIST IN ANGER AT HIM

GEE, HE WAS KINDA SKINNY

SHE IS NOW THROWING FOOD AT HIM

'IT' HAS TO GO!

21–27 28–34 35–41 42–48 49–51 52–58 59–65 66–72 73–79 80–84 85–91 92–98 99–105 106–112 113–118

PART I   PART II   PART III

PAGE NUMBER

After that pivotal scene when Gregor scares his mother half to death, Grete is done with him. Now she just throws food at him, and eventually she declares that this bug isn't Gregor at all—if it were him, he would have gone away on his own, and so now "[i]t has to go!" At the end, after Gregor has died, there is a last iteration in the *Gregor and Grete* series, a kind of bittersweet coda when she looks at his corpse and finally notices "[j]ust look how skinny he was."

The Z-Axis

On the series grid, I chose to chart three more series: *Grete's Music*, *Sister Emerges*, and *Lodgers*. I could have chosen others, such as which doors are locked, and whether the key is on the inside or the outside; or the furniture in the room being moved around, then taken out, then shoved back in; or Gregor's mother's escapist tendencies. Nor have I made note of all the household help, highlighted by the "bony Charwoman" who gets some of the best lines of the story, calling to Gregor, "Hey, over here, you old dung beetle! [. . .] Just look at the old dung beetle!"

The series I have chosen to chart are what I believe are the first nine in the top-down order of importance. How did I assess this? These nine series make sure that the questions are never all answered at the same time; they push the action forward. What emerges is an interesting phenomenon. As you may recall from high school geometry, the vertical rows on a series grid—what we have here as a succession of seven-page batches of the story—is called the y-axis. The x-axis is the one that stretches out horizontally to include the nine series, beginning with the two central series.

Why am I telling you this? Because following the logic that a series worth tracking has to ask a question and, that when one question is answered, another series has to ask a different one, there then exists a z-axis in addition to the x-axis and y-axis. This is actually a thing. If the x-axis is the width and the y-axis is the height, then the z-axis is the depth. On our series grid, it looks like this:

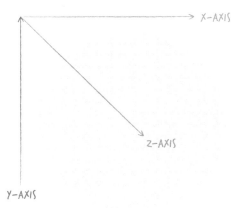

THE Z-AXIS
IN THE METAMORPHOSIS

The diagonal line, or z-axis, marked by the ruler, shows how newly occurring series keep the story moving. One thing leads to another, or, in the words of my colleague, Renee: "Bazinga! I knew it. The diagonals had it the whole time. So, this begs the question: Do I start reconstructing important series in order to augment the diagonal? And if so, then how?"

Well, drawing a series grid is a good start. In the case of the series grid we have created for Kafka's novella, the last point on our z-axis—that is, the farthest out on the x-axis and the farthest down on the y-axis—is the series where Gregor's *Sister Emerges*. This is where the diagonal push and pull of the series grid comes to its culmination; our awareness of this is helped by the fact that the last iteration of this series is literally the last line of the book. Having disposed of Gregor and taken the day off, the family boards a tram for the country. At the end of the ride, Gregor's sister "swiftly sprang to her feet and stretched her young body" (p. 118).

It wasn't always this way. In fact, in the first iteration of this series, we hear that Grete's care of Gregor marks the first time her parents aren't simply annoyed with her as a useless girl (p. 67). Because of the nature of this first iteration, we can presume several iterations of Grete being useless before the action of this story begins, represented by the dashed line at the beginning of the *Sister Emerges* series arc.

THE METAMORPHOSIS:

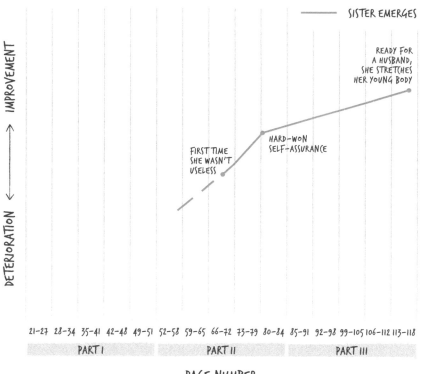

Gregor is partly responsible for helping his sister emerge; the level and type of care he requires contributes to her "hard won self-assurance." Unfortunately, this isn't the way he wanted his sister to emerge. He wanted to be the one who sent her to the conservatory to study her violin; she would then emerge only by knowing him as her benefactor. In a weird, semi-incestuous twist when this is no longer possible, Gregor daydreams of kidnapping her. But her emergence proves too strong, and she tells her parents that none of them should have to live like this. With Gregor gone, she blossoms almost as "a confirmation of their new dreams and good intentions" (p. 118).

The Theme of *The Metamorphosis*

We haven't talked very much about the theme of *The Metamorphosis* at this point. Another thing we have not done is reach prematurely for bigger and bigger series such as: *Hierarchy,* or *The Individual and the Collective*. Refraining from going for these bigger series is another tip of the cap to "Show, don't tell." Kafka doesn't tell us what his story is about—he *shows* us.

This opinion was shared by the German novelist Hermann Hesse. A young man had written to Hesse, inquiring whether certain symbols of Kafka's were religious, and about Kafka's relationship to Expressionist painting. Hesse wrote back to this reader, in part:

> Kafka's stories are not treatises about religious, metaphysical or moral problems—they are literary works. If a reader possesses the ability to really read a writer's works, namely without questions, without expecting intellectual or moral conclusions, and is simply ready to absorb what the author is presenting, those works will give the reader, in their own language, all the answers he is looking for.[*]

---

[*] Hermann Hesse, "Kafka Interpretations," Trans. Gerry Busch, 1997.

In one of the most classic disses in Kafka criticism, Hesse closes: "I felt that I owed you a reply, because you seemed to take the matter seriously."

We, too, take the matter seriously . . . to a point. When we go looking for the theme of *The Metamorphosis,* we are not likely to find it explicitly stated. Instead, we get red herrings such as *calm vs. chaos.* Upon finding out he has been transformed into an insect, Gregor admonishes himself that "he should behave calmly" and assist his family in enduring the inconveniences that will follow. Gregor's motto is that calm consideration "was far preferable to resolutions seized on in despair" (p. 29). His General Manager echoes this potential theme when he tells Gregor: "I have always known you as a calm, sensible person, and now it seems you've begun to permit yourself the most whimsical extravagances" (p. 36).

This isn't *the* theme, of course—this is a theme Kafka is making fun of, and, by looking at his gentle mockery, we can possibly see what he is really aiming at. The fact that Kafka doesn't tell us the one thing his novella is about doesn't mean he doesn't know. Instead, it means he has resisted the urge to put it in the story itself. It is your choice whether you put your one thing in your narrative to assist the reader's experience or you decide to obscure the bull's-eye of the series target.

It is true that we don't have Kafka's theme stated baldly for our review. I wonder if that might be a good thing because it forces us to graph together the four series arcs we have traced to this point, so that we can see what the author's story is "about" based on what he is actually doing. Creating a composite such as this is called plotting. As I mentioned, I'm okay with using "plot" as a verb, as long as we recognize that we will have to plot more than one narrative arc. Recalling that there is not one narrative arc—that there are only narrative arcs—leads us to a full expression of complexity—between oversimplifying things on the one hand and confusing everything on the other.

For the last image of this chapter, I have laid the four series arcs we have graphed one on top of the other. This is the visual representation of taking your top four series sentences from your order of importance and combining them until you get to two sentences and then the single-sentence expression of what your book is about (because your book can only be about one thing).

THE METAMORPHOSIS:
SERIES ARC 6

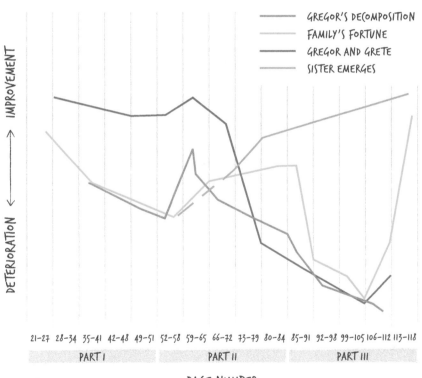

What conclusions can we draw now? *Gregor's Decomposition* and *Gregor and Grete* taper off at the bottom, while the *Family's Fortune* and

Sister Emerges series end at the top. One pair of series has deteriorated as far as imaginable, and the other pair has improved considerably. What lies in the middle is Kafka's theme.

It's a pretty wide gulf between the two series at the apex and those that fall to the bottom. This is the gulf between Gregor and the rest of his family once he has been labeled the I.P. (identified patient) in the dynamic. Gregor feels this, too: "Even though the others were no longer able to understand his words—though they had seemed to him clear enough, clearer than in the past, perhaps because his ear had grown accustomed to their sound [. . .]" (p. 40). While his family is debating *whether this is really Gregor?* and *whether Gregor will ever return to us?* Gregor has become aware that their perspective and his will never align again. Perhaps they never did.

Seen visually, the theme is what unites the four most important series. The disconnect between Gregor and his family is so profound he comes to the "opinion that he must by all means disappear" (p. 110). That is the theme of *The Metamorphosis,* and perhaps not coincidentally how Kafka saw writing: as a way to free himself by disappearing. In one of his famous fragments, *On Parables,* Kafka writes: "If you only followed the parables you yourselves would become parables and with that rid yourself of all your daily cares."*

My hope is that by watching me craft an extended series grid and six series arcs from scratch, you have been gained some confidence that you can do the same. You can, simply by focusing your attention on the necessary details, where, it turns out, the solutions are to be found as well.

---

*   *The Basic Kafka* (New York: Washington Square Press, 1979), 158.

Getting Hands-on:

Looking at your series grid, leave your central series and any time stamps as the first columns. After that, rearrange the columns of your series grid so that you can get a better glimpse of your z-axis: if a series begins later, or runs longer, move it farther to the right until you get the overall picture of how your narrative is evolving through a set of questions.

Next, take your most important series as determined by your top-down order of importance and draw their series arcs, overlaying them in as many groups as you find useful to more closely analyze their interactions, intersections, and collisions.

Taken together, the series target from Chapter Four, your complete series grid, and your set of series arcs will provide the clearest picture of your manuscript in process to this point. This picture can assist you as you go about making changes to benefit your story. And don't forget, when you change the story, change the information in your tools so they can continue to help you keep track.

The Metamorphosis: An Expanded Series Grid

Part	Page	Will Gregor Get to Work?	Gregor's Decomposition	Family's Fortune	Job Security
1	21-27	sees alarm clock, going to miss train		if it wasn't for parents' sake, he'd have given notice long ago	never been ill once in five years
	28-34	if he doesn't get out of bed, someone from the office will come			General Manager comes to visit, suspicion has been aroused
	35-41	can't get up to greet General Manager; opens lock with his jaws	injures himself, brown fluid runs out	sister crying because Gregor can't get up and parents will be hounded over ancient debt	keeping the cash payments? productivity has been unsatisfactory as of late
	42-48			Gregor is not in this job for life	not obstinate or a shirker, a victim of gossip?
2	49-51		scrapes himself on door, father shoves him in; bleeding profusely		
	52-58		left side one long contracting scar, limping outright; wounds have healed	feels great pride, but is it all coming to an end?	
	59-65		eating slows down	thought his father had retained nothing, instead a small nest egg remained	to be sure he could quit
	66-72		losing his eyesight	they are all going to find work	
	73-79		corrosive medicine engulfs him		
3	80-84		apple gets embedded in his back	father standing erect, gold buttons	
	85-91		wound Gregor receives from apple turns grievous, hobbles like an invalid	mother sewing ladies underthings, sister takes job as a salesgirl	
	92-98		stops eating, holds food in mouth only to spit it out again	household reduced, maid let go; can't move with Gregor in family	
	99-105		distances become great	one room let out to lodgers; Gregor's appearance drives them out	
	106-112		no longer capable of moving at all; dies	jobs pretty decent; taking the day off!	
	113-118				

Father's Violence	Gregor and Grete	Grete's Music	Sister Emerges	Lodgers
	sister only one to approach his condition with a lament			
clenches his fist with a horrible grimace	if only his sister were here, she was clever			
backs Gregor into his room brandishing walking stick, uttering wild hissing sounds				
	sister brings milk — always his favorite (now he only wants old cheese)			
	only Gregor's sister had remained close to him	Gregor planned to send her to the conservatory; she can play the violin quite movingly		
	she replaces the armchair where he likes it			
	Gregor's appearance horrifies his mother; Grete raises her fist		holds Gregor expertise; hard-won self assurance	
father throws the apples	(Grete's allegiance transferred to the father)			
	sister now throwing food at him			
		couldn't remember having heard the violin all this time		
		music brings Gregor out of his room; music stops		seemed to only tolerate Grete's playing; spy Gregor
	It has to go! How could it be Gregor?			
	he went such a long time without eating anything		Grete ready for a husband, swiftly springs to her feet and stretches her young body	father orders the lodgers out

The Three Tools of Book Architecture

B ack when I was writing *BYB*, I wanted to use *The Metamorphosis* as an example, but I was counseled rightly to use something shorter and more approachable, so I chose "The Ugly Duckling," by Hans Christian Andersen. Now we have come full circle to the end of my second book on writing—and there are only going to be two. We do have one more chapter together, however, in which we will discuss the three tools of Book Architecture a final time.

A natural question to ask at this point is: When should I break out the three tools? This question recalls our discussion from Chapter Five of the outliners versus the pantsers. There, we said that most writers are probably both: they keep an outline of some form going somewhere, while, at the same time, they write by the seat of their pants, even when just pushing a scene further than they expected as they discover the unknown.

Only a very few number of writers can write a complete outline first and then write their whole piece. For the rest of us, that's not really the way it works. Writers sometimes come to me with these complex outlines before they've ever written a word, and I have to pull out this E. M. Forster quote: "How can I know what I think, until I see what I say?"

But that doesn't mean you should never apply analytical methods. You might take the time to use one (or more) of the three tools of Book Architecture between drafts in order to reflect on what you have done in the previous draft. Or you might wait until you are suffering "draft fatigue"—that is, when it becomes hard, in the middle of a draft, to discern the way forward—and take a step back instead to find another angle while you ask yourself important orienting questions.

It isn't as though the three tools are magic. Some of the answers to your questions will be found only in the writing, which brings us back to pantsing, and around it goes in a great big circle.

Using the Series Target

Thus far we have confined our discussion to examples that are out there for anyone to read or view: short stories, well-known films, etc. I have refrained from using my clients' work because digging deeper into what certain decisions meant for their narratives would be like me telling you about a party that you couldn't attend. But at this point, I do want to bring in a few visuals produced by people just like us to clarify and advance a few concepts.

The series target was first presented in full in Chapter Four. By putting our series sentences in a top-down order of importance, we came up with a working or provisional theme and then put that theme in the bull's-eye of an archery target. We then placed series on the target closer to or farther from the theme based on perceived relevance. We also noticed how certain series tended to cluster together and how some series miss the target altogether, meaning that either we have to change the theme or we have to challenge ourselves to leave this material behind once and for all.

Below is a photograph of Jeanette's archery target. Jeanette has courage. Not only has she identified those arrows that didn't hit the target, those laying in the hay, as it were, but she has gone the extra step of tagging them with green stickies, officially weighing them down so they will never rise back up into her draft as if they belong.

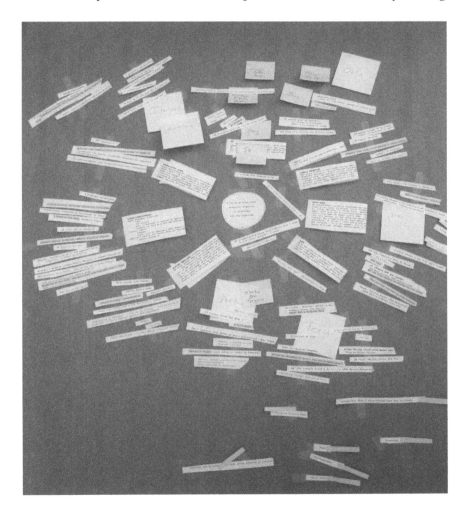

When you place your theme in the bull's-eye and a series doesn't even hit the target, you know you are looking at a "darling" in William

Faulkner's famous phrase.* It could be a short story lurking inside your novel like an enemy warrior inside a Trojan horse. Or it could be a passage or a point that was truly inspired, well designed, and beautifully executed but that will not make the whole greater than the sum of its parts. And so it must go.

Using the Series Arc

Once we know that all our series belong to the same book, as it were, we can begin to examine their relationships to each other more closely. In the last chapter, we saw how drawing series arcs and then combining them can provide a lot of insight in terms of the meaning you are generating, whether you overlay two series on top of each other, or four, or all of them. But you can also draw a series arc just to get one series right—to make it crisp and conscious instead of muddy with missing iterations.

Tye has been brave enough to volunteer one such series arc, which he drew when he just couldn't figure out what was going wrong. In brief, this series details how the main character of his novel-in-progress, Eli, feels about his now deceased wife, Julia. I teased Tye, that every time he didn't seem to know what to do, he just went back to Eli reflecting on Julia, and it was reminiscent of Forrest Gump (if you saw that movie, you probably remember the main character filling empty space at repeated intervals by saying ". . . mostly I just thought about Jenny . . ." with absolutely no provocation).

Tye agreed to put the Julia series to the test. Instead of labeling his vertical axis from IMPROVEMENT to DETERIORATION, he labeled it based on Eli's feelings toward Julia. Thus his scale ran from: *very positive – positive – slightly positive – slightly negative – negative – very*

---

* Faulkner's full advice runs: "In writing, you must kill all your darlings." He borrowed the concept from Sir Arthur Quiller-Couch: "Whenever you feel an impulse to perpetrate a piece of exceptionally fine writing, obey it—whole-heartedly—and delete it before sending your manuscript to press. Murder your darlings."

negative – wow, what a b!@#!!* When he crafted this series arc, he found several things. First of all, he had fifty-five iterations. Fifty-five is *a lot.* I'm all for repetition and variation, but this seriously risks overload. Second, emotions come from riding the ups and downs of a series arc, but we need to be able to experience where we are first, which is almost impossible with this kind of yo-yo effect:

CONCLUSION:
TYE'S SERIES ARC

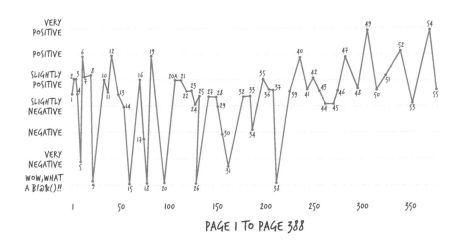

PAGE 1 TO PAGE 388

You can chart as many series arcs as you think might be of benefit for your process. As I mentioned, you may even decide to pursue all of them and put them on the same graph. Then, if you take a step back and squint a little, you might see one narrative arc as opposed to a bunch of individual arcs. You might have one overall narrative arc—that would make the people with a formula happy—or you might not. We have seen examples of both in this book. Since the subtitle here is how to plot (and outline) without a formula, all I'm saying is that when we regard our collection of series arcs all together, we might be tempted to call what we have created a "plot." But if we do use this word, we must, at the same time, acknowledge that a "plot" is something you *achieve,* such as unity or enlightenment. A series, on the other hand, is something you *do.*

Using the Series Grid

Whenever you identify a series in your work, you give it a name, assign it a type, and identify its iterations. You can then either graph it as a series arc or assign it a column in your series grid—or both. Both tools can help you figure out where you are missing iterations or have them in excess, and both can help you create foreshadowing and build suspense. The series arc is especially good at revealing the emotional movement of a series, while the series grid excels at keeping everything together. With all the series on one grid, you can more easily find the right balance to strike in a given scene, where to go more in depth, and how to create the key scenes where everything feels like it is coming together for the emotional payoff.

As Jenn put her series grid together, she said the tool helped give her confidence that she would be able to continue her major series all the way through to the end. It shone a light on the chapters that had a relative void of action (fewer series interacting, intersecting, and colliding). It helped her put a finger on what was bothering her about one character's lack of a specific resolution and the fact that another character's punishment didn't seem to fit her crime.

I'm not expecting you to be able to read the details pictured in the part of Jenn's series grid pictured on the next page, and, due to the practical consideration of not wanting to analyze her entire novel at this point in our work together, we can't really examine how she set up her rows and columns. If you want, we can go into the fact that she cut up her big poster board to send to me in the mail, complete with Post-it notes to show what order to lay out the individual panels, *and then didn't even keep a copy.*

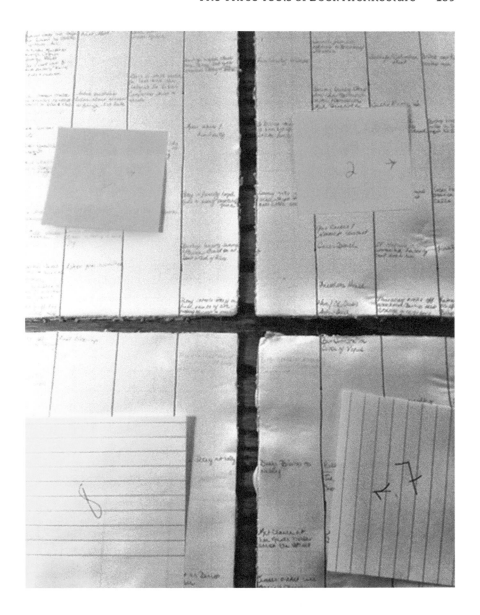

No, the point is that people do this stuff. I did it, for this book. You can use the Book Architecture Method for nonfiction as well. I used it on my first book; at the time, my editor, Maria, emailed me: "I just wanted you to know that you don't have any major revising ahead of you. And that's an especially good thing, since we'd have big trouble on our hands if it wasn't a successful manuscript, no?"

At the end of this chapter, I have reproduced the series grid I put together for this book. Although it is possible to separate a work of nonfiction into scenes by drilling down to the level of various subheads, I simply set up my rows by batches of three to four pages, just as we did with Kafka's novella.

For the columns, I chose which series to track based on some of the variables we have been discussing. Some series, like *Repetition and Variation* or the *Five Components of Series*, I kept track of because I wanted to make sure to get them in there a lot. These series didn't really go through any logical development; it was more like showing different sides of the same question.

I kept track of some series such as the *Central Series* so that I could gently introduce it in Chapter One, develop it a little in Chapter Two, and then bring it to full fruition in Chapter Three. There's only so much you can get across at once, and literally being able to look across at everything a chapter contains helps you assess how much is too much. I kept track of the *Series Arc* for much the same reason; in Chapter One, we promise that these arcs will get progressively fancier, and they do: from two points on a line, to arcs made up of between three and fifteen points, to layering two series arcs on top of each other, to layering four arcs on top of each other.[*]

Starting this book with how four narrative arcs reveal the theme of Kafka's novella would have risked the reader's disorientation. There is an art to knowing when to introduce something, and this art is

---

[*] On a related note, I didn't keep track of the evolutions within the "Getting Hands-on" sections at the end of each chapter because it was obvious they needed to develop, and it was easy to find the last iteration.

supported by the tool of the series grid. Of course, you want to mention as many things as you can right off the bat in the Introduction, and, therefore, the Introduction in non-fiction does function as a kind of key scene. But you also want to take advantage of the z-axis; in my case, once I felt I had the basics of series established, I introduced a new major wrinkle with each succeeding chapter: the central series, the series target, the expanded series grid, and so on. Knowing where I was on the z-axis also gave me information I needed for the title of that chapter. At the same time, there is a danger in introducing series too far into the work. The *Z-Axis* series itself isn't introduced until the last chapter (and reiterated in this one). Was that too late? I'll let you be the judge.

Using this series grid is how I outlined this book without using a formula. I started it in the middle of my work, somewhere between the outliners and the pantsers. It helped with decisions, such as how far apart the iterations of a series could be while still expecting people to remember what I was talking about. Could I just touch on something, or did I have to hit it a little harder? But it also led to breakthroughs for me. In fact, it was why I wrote Chapter Seven the way I did, because now I knew what I wanted the book to be about, and I broke through to doing what I knew needed to be done—and what I wanted to do—at the same time. Awesome feeling.

That's why I don't regard using these three tools as "analytical" as opposed to "creative." You're still going to get the same rate of good ideas per hour (whatever that rate happens to be). They may be different kinds of ideas about your narrative, but they will prove just as valuable to its completion.

Okay, that's it. Good luck, and let me know how it goes. And I'm sure it's going to go great.

BOOK ARCHITECTURE:
A SERIES GRID FOR THIS BOOK

	THE THREE TOOLS					FIVE COMPONENTS OF SERIES				
	SERIES ARC	SERIES GRID	SERIES TARGET	NO FORMULA	SERIES IS THE NEW PLOT	SERIES NAME	TYPES OF SERIES	HOW MANY ITERATIONS?	SERIES SENTENCES	EVERY SERIES ASKS A QUESTION
INTRODUCTION	●	●	●							
	●	●	●	●	●		●			
						●	●	●	●	●
CHAPTER ONE: CORDUROY		●			●					●
	●	●					●	●		●
		●								
CHAPTER TWO: THE GREAT GATSBY		●				●	●	●	●	
						●	●		●	
	●					●	●			●
						●				
CHAPTER THREE: SLUMDOG MILLIONAIRE		●			●					●
										●
CHAPTER FOUR: THE SOCIAL NETWORK		●			●	●	●	●	●	●
	●	●					●	●		●
		●								
CHAPTER FIVE: HARRY POTTER, V		●	●							
	●	●			●	●			●	
	●	●	●	●	●					
CHAPTER SIX: CATCH-22		●						●		
		●		●						
CHAPTER SEVEN: THE METAMORPHOSIS	●	●								
	●	●				●	●			
	●	●				●				
	●									
CONCLUSION	●		●	●	●					
		●		●						

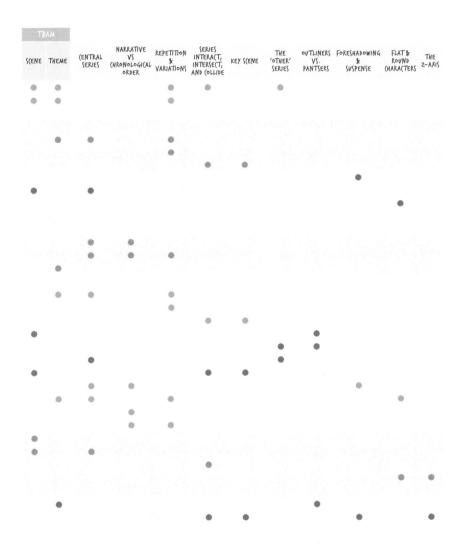

Works Cited

Beaufoy, Simon. *Slumdog Millionaire: The Shooting Script*. New York: Newmarket Press, 2008.

Brooks, Larry. *Story Engineering*. Cincinnati: Writer's Digest Books, 2011.

Fitzgerald, F. Scott. *The Great Gatsby*. New York: Scribner, 2004.

Freeman, Don. "Corduroy." New York: Puffin/Penguin, 1976.

Heller, Joseph. "The Art of Fiction." *Paris Review* 60 (Winter 1974).

Heller, Joseph. *Catch-22*. New York: Simon & Schuster, 2004.

Hesse, Hermann. "Kafka Interpretations." Trans. Gerry Busch. 1997. http://everything2.com/title/Kafka+Interpretations Accessed January 12, 2015.

Horwitz, Stuart. *Blueprint Your Bestseller: Organize and Revise Any Manuscript with the Book Architecture Method*. New York: Perigee/Penguin, 2013.

Kafka, Franz. *The Basic Kafka*. Intro. Erich Heller. New York: Washington Square Press, 1979.

Kafka, Franz. *The Metamorphosis*. Trans. Susan Bernofsky. New York: W.W. Norton, 2014.

Politzer, Heinz. *Franz Kafka: Parable and Paradox*. Ithaca, NY: Cornell University Press, 1966.

Quiller-Couch, Sir Arthur. *On the Art of Writing*. New York: Capricorn Books, 1916. Reprinted 1961.

Renton, Jennie. "The Story Behind the Potter Legend." *Sydney Morning Herald*, Oct. 28, 2001.

Rowling, J.K. *Harry Potter and the Order of the Phoenix*. New York: Scholastic, 2013.

Rowling, J.K. *J.K. Rowling Interview*. By *Scholastic*, Feb. 3, 2000.

Rowling, J.K. "World Exclusive Interview with J K Rowling," *South West News Service*, July 8, 2000.

Steinbeck, John. *Journal of a Novel: The* East of Eden *Letters*. New York: Penguin, 1990.

Sorkin, Aaron. *The Social Network*. Culver City, CA: Sony Pictures, 2010.

The Social Network (Two-Disc Collector's Edition). Directed by David Fincher. 2010. Culver City, CA: Sony Pictures, 2011. DVD.

Tobias, Ronald. *20 Master Plots: And How to Build Them*. Cincinnati: Writer's Digest Books, 1993.

Acknowledgments

My daily life travels in the orbit of three women: my wife, Bonnie Kane, and my two daughters, Fifer and Bodhi. I simply can't imagine having the centeredness and momentum to write this book without your love.

My once and future editor, Maria Gagliano: your wit is only matched by your work ethic. Perhaps the ~~scariest~~ most inspiring thing about you is your ability to answer my questions without them ever leaving my head.

My co-author of Chapter Five and compadre throughout, C.S. Plocher: thank you for your dedication and aesthetic intelligence. Now how's about using all of that and finishing your book?

The incredible visuals in this book are the work of Molly Regan of Logica Design. Molly, you have one serious eye. And you also take under-promising and over-delivering to a *whole* other level.

My beta readers who believed I could handle the truth: Luann Castle, Michael Coffino, Tasneem Zehra Hussain, Windy Lynn Harris, Chloe Marsala, Renee Rivers, and Terry Treece: each of you has contributed something so seminal to this work sometimes I think it's folly that my name is the only one on the cover.

My three colleagues who allowed their work-in-progress to be praised/delicately lampooned in the Conclusion, Jennifer Mancuso,

Jeanette Stokes, and Tye Tyson: thank you for letting us in before company is technically supposed to arrive.

Many individuals submitted to a grueling questionnaire as I was rounding the bend from Book One to Book Two. In addition to those mentioned above, thank you for your insights: Pamela Coleman, Ray Daniel, Lori Hughes, Scott Moon, Jennifer Salcido, Medb Sichko, and Jesse Turland.

For the book itself that you are holding, I would like to thank Michele DeFilippo and Ronda Rawlins at 1106 Design; Linda Feldman, our copyeditor-in-chief; and Louann Pope all for working with some scary turnaround times.

Looking ahead to the Book Architecture tour, I know I will want to thank the guy with more talent in his little finger . . . Dave Stebenne, for outfitting me with stop-action short films that make me look like a pro. Respect also to the rhythm section of Art Don't Pay, Tim Ison and Rob Degnan, for backing us up.

Finally, for providing support both specific and atmospheric: Ted Heller, Chloe Morse-Harding, Heidrun Schmidt, Anne Woodrum— and anyone who's let me sneak on to their A-List...you know who you are.

About the Author

S TUART HORWITZ is the founder and principal of Book Architecture, a firm of independent editors based in Providence, New York, and Boston (www.BookArchitecture.com).

He developed the Book Architecture Method over fifteen years of helping writers get from first draft to final draft. In the process, those same writers have become authors: signing with top literary agencies and landing book deals at coveted publishing houses.

Book Architecture's clients have reached the bestseller list in both fiction and nonfiction, and have appeared on *The Oprah Winfrey Show, Today, The Tonight Show,* and in the most prestigious journals in their respective fields.

Horwitz's first book, *Blueprint Your Bestseller: Organize and Revise Any Manuscript with the Book Architecture Method* (Penguin/Perigee) was named one of the best books about writing in 2013 by *The Writer* magazine.

He lives in Rhode Island with his wife and two daughters.

CPSIA information can be obtained
at www.ICGtesting.com
Printed in the USA
BVHW02s1359190418
513692BV00006B/39/P